F

ONE OF A KIND, WORKIN' ON A FULL HOUSE

GARTH BROOKS

RICK MITCHELL

A Fireside Book
Published by Simon & Schuster
New York   London   Toronto   Sydney   Tokyo   Singapore

For Lori and Chelsea

FIRESIDE
Simon & Schuster Building
Rockefeller Center
1230 Avenue of the Americas
New York, New York 10020

FIRESIDE and colophon are registered trademarks
of Simon & Schuster Inc.

Designed by Stanley S. Drate, Folio Graphics Co., New York

Produced by Rapid Transcript/March Tenth, Inc.

Manufactured in the United States of America

10   9   8   7   6   5   4   3   2   1

Library of Congress Cataloging-in-Publication Data is available.

ISBN: 0-671-79688-7

CONTENTS

ACKNOWLEDGMENTS

Without these special people, this book would not have happened, or might have been far more difficult to finish:

Lori Sumako, Mom and Joe, Sandy Choron, Chuck Adams, Rachel Burd, Jory Farr, Dave Marsh, Keith Moerer, Ronnie Pugh, Jack Loftis, Tony Pederson, Susan Bischoff, Jane Marshall, Melissa Aguilar, Marty Racine, Dave Ritz, Clem and Peggy Mundy, Bubba and Sandy Pedrazas, Holly Crawford.

I also would like to thank those important folks who consented to interviews with me:

Gene Cranfill, Kathy Brown, Rene Huckaba, Larry LoBaugh, Bea Johnson, Todd Johnson, Dale Pierce, Jim Bolding, Jeff Fair, Mike Platt, Dolly Bloodworth, Vince Dudenhoeffer, Eddie Watkins, Jimmy LaFave, Tom Skinner, Greg Jacobs, Bob Childers, Amy Kurland, Pat Alger, Pam Lewis, Joe Harris, Maria Thornton, Lynn Shults, Allen Reynolds, Mark Miller, Waylon Jennings, Clint Black, Jimmy Bowen, Tony Arata, Mark Chesnutt, Bill Ivey, and Garth Brooks.

The following writers and publications provided information that proved invaluable:

Michael McCall ("Long may he run . . ."), *Request*, *The Yukon Review*, Bob Millard, *Country Music*, *The San Francisco Chronicle*, Rob Tannenbaum, *Rolling Stone*, Jim Jerome, *People*, *The Orlando Sentinel*, Jim Lewis, *El Reno Tribune*, Jack Hurst, *Chicago Tribune*, *Tulsa World*, *ASCAP in Action*, *The Atlanta Journal*, John Morthland, *The Journal of Country Music*, *The Jackson Clarion-Ledger*, *USA Today*, *Performance*, Bob Oermann, *The Nashville Tennessean*, Jay Orr, *The Nashville Banner*, Jill Nelson, *USA Weekend*, Celeste Gomes, *Billboard*, Karen Schoemer, *The New York Times*, Mike Greenblatt, *Modern Screen Yearbook*, *Forbes*, *Time*, *Stereo Review*, *The Dallas Morning News*, *The Believer*.

JUST AN OLD, FAT, BALD COWBOY

"When I look in the mirror, I still see the same bum I always did."

Garth Brooks was singing "The Dance," the dramatic ballad that catapulted him from cowboy-hat-wearing contender to country superstar, to a crowd of young women standing in front of the stage at Houston's Woodlands Pavilion. After one adoring female fan handed Brooks a long-stemmed rose, anyone with a good seat could read his lips. "I love you, too," he said in a stage whisper.

The woman's male companion leaned over to his buddy and muttered, "I don't get it. Hell, he's just an old, fat, bald cowboy."

When I later relayed this observation to Brooks, he chuckled. "I've said that myself," he admitted, as his tour bus rolled down a desolate stretch of West Texas highway somewhere outside of San Angelo.

"I happen to share the same thought. I kid you not. Let's face it, heartthrob is not in the vocabulary for an artist like me. I could understand it if I looked in the mirror and saw a man that was handsome and well-built. I see that in George, Clint, and Alan. But I just don't see it in me. When I look in the mirror, I still see the same bum I always did."

So how is it that this "old, fat, bald cowboy" from Oklahoma has become the biggest musical star in America? Why Garth Brooks? That's the multiplatinum question many people in the music industry—not to mention the rest of the world—are asking themselves.

In little more than three years, Garth Brooks's career has blasted off to boldly go where no man in a cowboy hat has gone before. Sales of Garth's five albums have exceeded twenty million—by far the most of any American artist so far in this decade.

In September 1991, Brooks's *Ropin' the Wind* became the first country album ever to enter both the country and pop charts at Number 1. In late '91 and early '92, the album successfully beat back challenges by some of pop's biggest names, including Guns N' Roses, Hammer, U2, and Michael Jackson. A year after its release, *Ropin' the Wind* is still holding strong in the Top 10, with total sales of more than seven million.

What's more, Brooks's previous album, *No Fences*, also has topped eight million sales and is still in the Top 10 on the country chart and Top 40 on the pop chart, more than two years after its release.

Garthmania continued unabated with the August 1992 release of *Beyond the Season*, a Christmas album. Advance retail orders exceeded 1.6 million—an all-time record for a Christmas album. Brooks is donating one dollar from the sale of each copy of *Beyond the Season* to Feed the Children, a Christian charity based in Oklahoma City.

Brooks's latest album, *The Chase*, was released in September 1992, just before this book went to press.

Brooks's 1992 tour, which began in June, has sold out everywhere it's gone. In several cities, the demand for tickets was so intense that it knocked the phone lines out of commission on the day the tickets went on sale. Nor has Garthmania been confined to the traditional country strongholds in the South and West. Brooks sold out the 16,000-seat Los Angeles Forum in 14 minutes, the New York State Fair in Syracuse in under an hour, and the 27,500-seat Chicago World Amphitheater in one hour and 21 minutes.

Before we go any further, some clarification is in order here. At thirty, Brooks certainly isn't old, not when compared to octogenarian country patriarch Roy Acuff, or fifty-something rock icon Bob Dylan. A beefy ex-jock, he's not really fat, either. True, his hair is thinning a bit on top, but he's not uptight about it. And while Brooks is the epitome of a modern-day cowboy singer in a black hat and boots, he's no rodeo cowboy. In fact, he's admitted to a childhood fear of horses.

Brooks might still see the same bum in the mirror he always did, but chances are it's a more expensive mirror that he's gazing into these days. In 1991, Garth and his wife, Sandy, purchased a home on a hill outside of Nashville previously owned by former mayor Richard Fulton. The purchase price of the home was estimated by the *Nashville Tennessean* at close to a half-million dollars, with an additional remodeling bill set at around $400,000. (They've added a baby room done in a Disney motif for Taylor Mayne Pearl Brooks, born July 8, 1992.) Brooks also reportedly purchased a $640,000 estate for his parents near Oklahoma City.

Brooks claims he nearly fainted during renegotiations on his current record deal. "I had to stop for five minutes so I could go out and breathe because of the ungodly amounts they were talkin' about," he said. "My head was spinnin'."

Remarkably, unlike previous country crossover successes from Johnny Cash to Dolly Parton, Brooks has achieved his across-the-board popularity without exposure on pop radio stations or video channels. Yet, the Garth Brooks phenomenon extends far beyond the traditional country audience. All across the nation, young girls who two years ago were gravitating to New Kids on the Block are buying Wrangler jeans and Roper boots and "going country" for Brooks's concerts. Garth's fans range from Texas teenyboppers to Florida grandmothers, and from rodeo cowboys in Oklahoma to college prepsters in California.

"I see it all the time," Brooks says. "Some kid will pull up playing the hardest rock stuff I can stand to listen to. And then I'll look in the truck and see my album or [Strait's] *Chill of an Early Fall* sitting there. It makes you feel good that country music is growing, whether I'm a part of it or not."

Still, Brooks portrays himself as just an average guy blessed with a combination of talent and luck. He professes to be as mystified as that poor guy at the concert by the overwhelming adulation he's received.

"I'm thankful for the success, but I really don't have a clue why it happened to me," he has said. "Because what I deserve and what I've gotten are totally off balance. Right now, if this world was split where part of 'em went to heaven, and part of 'em went to hell, you'd probably be seeing me right on the front line of people going to hell. All I can say is that it's divine intervention."

Garth might be right, but his story may provide other more tangible explanations. From his childhood and college years in Oklahoma to his arrival in Nashville as a struggling singer-songwriter and subsequent success beyond anyone's wildest dreams, Brooks's music and personal values were shaped by his upbringing. There's also something of a love story—between Garth and his fans, of course, but also between Garth and his wife, Sandy.

But to fully appreciate the nature of Brooks's appeal, it's necessary to watch him in live performance. In a one-year period between February 1990 and February 1991, Garth went from playing a small, five hundred–seat nightclub on his first concert visit to Houston to driving sixty thousand Texans into a whistlin', woofin', foot-stompin' frenzy at the Houston Livestock Show and Rodeo, the top-grossing country music event in the world.

Garth compares the thrill he gets from being onstage to sexual excitement. "A great concert is like any great sex, where you get wild and frenzied, then turn that around quick to something gentle, tender, and slow, and then get wild and crazy again, and just keep doing that over and over until one of you drops dead. If you've done what a sexual partner should, then that woman should live the rest of her life saying, 'Damn! Sex is good!' That's the way it is with music."

To paraphrase one of his hits, Garth Brooks truly is "one of a kind, workin' on a full house."

On May 31, 1992, Garth returned to Yukon, Oklahoma, for the dedication ceremony in which Garth Brooks Boulevard was officially named.

GARTH BROOKS BLVD.

"Whoever said you couldn't go home wasn't from Yukon, Oklahoma."

On May 31, 1992, Garth Brooks returned to his hometown of Yukon, Oklahoma. The city had named a street after him and invited him to a dedication ceremony in the auditorium of Yukon High School. A capacity crowd of four thousand citizens came out to honor their local hero, including many of Garth's old friends and family members, an Elvis impersonator, and Oklahoma governor David Walters.

Yukon schools superintendent Darrell Hill presented Garth with a plaque on behalf of the Yukon Public Schools Foundation for Excellence. "He has set a standard of excellence that will give every kid in this town something to shoot for," said Hill. "It's very exciting. It might be the best place to be in the world today. Not too many communities could boast of having the two-time [Country Music Association] Entertainer of the Year."

Yukon mayor Dave O'Bannon read a proclamation declaring May 31, 1992, "Garth Brooks Appreciation Day" in Yukon. He gave Garth three street signs—one that read "Garth Brooks Blvd.," one for his wife reading "Sandy Brooks Ave.," and one for his (at the time) unborn daughter, "Taylor Mayne Pkwy." The Yukon Chamber of Commerce gave Garth a T-shirt and a blanket, also for Taylor.

After two hours of speeches and local entertainment, the crowd grew restless and began to chant, "We want Garth! We want Garth!" When the star appeared from backstage and stepped into the spotlight in the darkened auditorium, girls ran toward the stage and threw roses at his feet. "He's hot, he's good-lookin', and he's a man made for Wranglers," said one fifteen-year-old female fan. "Plus, I go to his school!"

Garth's reaction was typical of the comparatively humble, down-to-earth manner in which he has approached his superstar celebrity status in the past two years. He laughed as a young member of a children's choir attempted to break a guitar over his knee, "just like Garth," and shed a few tears during the choir's rendition of his spiritual anthem "The River."

When his turn to speak finally arrived, Garth told the audience, "A lot of people talk about how small towns drag them down and they keep trying to get out from them. But there's

something small towns have that big cities seem to [lack]—
and that's just good old common sense and good old good-
heartedness.''

Garth Brooks Boulevard runs past Yukon High School, from which
Garth graduated in 1980. In the distance you can see the water tower that
reads ''Yukon—Home of Garth Brooks,'' above a listing of the years in
which Yukon High athletic teams have won divisional state championships.
The street previously was called Cemetery Road, because it also runs past
the town's cemetery. A local joke has it the cemetery will be renamed
Friends in Low Places.

At a press conference earlier in the day covered by the *Yukon Review*,
Garth said he was truly honored by the dedication ceremony. ''In high
school, with the speed limit out here the way it is, I paid for enough tickets
to pay for the street, so it feels good to have my name on it,'' he joked. Then
he turned serious. ''This business is noted for the awards that it gives, but
it's things like this that are really cool because there's only one Yukon, Oklahoma, and that makes me feel very special.''

*G*arth in the fourth grade

Someone asked Garth what else the city could do for him now that he
has a street and a water tower in his name. His answer drew chuckles from
civic leaders. ''I don't know, but I'd like to see the town remain as Yukon.''
As for the fans who stood in line for up to three hours in a light Sunday
morning drizzle waiting to get in the auditorium, Garth said he was puzzled.
''If I was waiting out there in the rain, it would be for somebody a helluva
lot more special than me.''

Governor Walters presented Garth with an award on behalf of the state's
Highway Safety Office for his work promoting the use of seatbelts. In 1991,
Garth taped two radio public service announcements urging listeners to
buckle up. Walters credited the announcements with helping to decrease
traffic fatalities in Oklahoma in the past year.

''If you feel that lump in your throat, you know that's Oklahoma pride,''
Walters said. ''It's clear that [Garth] doesn't pay lip service to being an Oklahoman—he's proud of it. He takes every opportunity he can to say hello to
the folks back home.''

After Walters told the crowd that Yukon was ''the place to be today,''
Garth took it one step further. ''The governor was kind of right except everyday is a day to be in Yukon,'' he said. ''Whoever said you couldn't go home
wasn't from Yukon, Oklahoma. It feels different when I'm not here in town.
But when I come to town everything feels the same. I'm still the same bum
I was when I was here, and people still treat me like me. This is *home*, and
that's the way home should be.''

Immediately after the dedication ceremony, Garth and his band left for
Denver, Colorado, where he opened his 1992 tour on June 2.

*I*n the seventh grade,
1975

A big part of who Garth Brooks is and what he stands for can be attributed to the traditional family and religious values instilled in him as a kid
growing up in Yukon. Although he now lives in Nashville and tours around

A *Little League photo, taken when Garth was in the fifth grade. That's him in the first row; he's Number 60.*

T*he eighth grade football team at Yukon Junior High. Garth is Number 12: bottom row, second from left.*

the world, he carries those values with him everywhere he goes. And if he's ever tempted to forget where he came from, Garth's got his sister Betsy, brother Kelly, and lifelong friend Mickey Webber around to remind him. Betsy plays bass in Garth's band, Stillwater; Kelly is Garth's tour accountant; Mickey is his road manager.

"I surrounded myself with people who knew me long before I happened," says Brooks. "So if I start acting different, man, they'll square me in a minute."

Gene Cranfill, the associate superintendent of schools in Yukon, can remember when Garth was learning to play the banjo in high school. Cranfill, a singer, often was asked to perform at community functions. One of Garth's first public performances was backing him up at a Future Farmers of America banquet. They did Johnny Cash's "Dirty Old Egg-Suckin' Dog."

Like many in Yukon, Cranfill is proud of his famous former pupil, both for the amazing level of success he's achieved and how gracefully he's handled it so far. "The thing that impresses me is when I see him on television and hear him talk, he's still Garth Brooks, the kid I knew in school," Cranfill said. "He's not just saying things. He's real."

Yukon bills itself as "one of America's safest cities" and "the finest hometown in Oklahoma." Located in the geographical center of the state about fifteen miles west of Oklahoma City, Yukon is a bedroom community of about twenty thousand dotted by city parks, drive-in hamburger stands, and Little League diamonds. The town takes pride in its highly rated school system and low crime rate.

In the eighth grade, 1976

A historical marker in Mulvey's Park denotes where the legendary Chisholm Trail passed through the present city limits. In the late nineteenth century, cowboys drove millions of Texas longhorn cattle up the Chisholm Trail across Oklahoma to the stockyards and railroads in Kansas. Every August, Yukon hosts the Chisholm Trail Festival, featuring a cattle drive and a rodeo.

Many of the first settlers in Yukon were Czech farmers, and the local Czech Hall has hosted country-western and polka dances on weekends for as long as anybody can remember. The tallest building in town is still the abandoned grain mill on Main Street, which is why the high school team is known as the Millers.

But from the late sixties through the seventies, Yukon's population roughly tripled. This rapid increase was largely the result of "white flight" from Oklahoma City; Yukon's population is more than 95 percent white.

As a small farming town that's become a big city suburb, Yukon's growth parallels the evolution of country music in recent decades. What once was considered "hillbilly" music, beloved by "simple" country folk and scorned by "sophisticated" urban dwellers, has become the preferred format for a sizable and growing segment of suburban radio listeners, according to several recent surveys. Garth's own music reflects this suburban baby-boomer outlook in its blend of traditional country instrumentation and vocals with contemporary lyrics and rock and roll energy.

Yukon was still a small town when the Brooks family moved there in the mid-1960s. Troyal Garth Brooks was born in Tulsa on February 7, 1962, the youngest of six children. He has four brothers and one sister. His father, Troyal Raymond Brooks, has worked as a draftsman for Union Oil for more than thirty-five years, and Garth jokingly has referred to his family heritage as "oil-field trash."

All the Brooks boys played high school football as well as other sports, and their parents seldom missed a game. Rene Huckaba, athletic director at Yukon High, remembers Ray Brooks as "a pretty tough kinda guy. I mean in a good way. You think of a typical Western kinda guy—an athletic, ex-Marine, don't-cry, don't-show-any-pain kinda guy."

While Ray might have been stern and tough on the outside, his children never had any doubts that he loved and cared about them. Garth has said of his father, "He was a Golden Gloves [boxing] champ in the Marines in Korea, but he's the softest-hearted man you ever could meet. If I could be like any man in the world, it would be him. He had six kids and paid for every one of them to go to college, although he never made over twenty thousand dollars a year until recently."

Garth elaborated on his father's character and what he learned from him in an interview with writer Bob Millard published in *Country Music* magazine:

"If I could wrap my dad up in two words, it would be thundering tenderness. He's a man with the shortest temper I ever saw, and at the same time he's got the biggest heart. Some of the greatest conflicts are not between two people but between one person and himself. He knows what's right and he doesn't have any tolerance for what isn't right, but at the same time he is so forgiving. I learned from him that you gotta be thankful for what you got and treat people like you want to be treated. My dad drilled that into my head all my life. We're a lot alike in that way."

But if Garth grew up worshiping his father and wanting to be like him, he inherited much of his emotional makeup as well as his musical inclinations from his mother. In the early fifties, Colleen Carroll Brooks had been a featured singer on Red Foley's Ozark Jubilee show in Springfield, Missouri. She recorded a few sides for Capitol Records before giving up her career to start a family. She is an outspoken extrovert by nature, a flamboyant dresser who laughs and cries easily in public. This last is a trait shared by Garth, sometimes to his embarrassment.

The townspeople will tell you that Colleen has never been shy about expressing her opinions. For example, if she disagreed with a coach's decision to pull one of her sons out of a game, the coach could expect to get an earful from our Mrs. Brooks after the game. "Colleen is a nice person," says Cranfill. "It's just that you don't have to wonder what she's thinking."

Although she repeatedly tried to dissuade him from pursuing a career in music, Garth has said that his mother is the inspiration for his musical ambitions. Her kids used to ask her why she never tried to get back in the business. She never gave a satisfactory answer.

"She's probably got the best voice of any woman I've ever heard," he told a *San Francisco Chronicle* reporter in 1990. "That was kind of like a secret, and a drive behind this whole thing. To really pick up where she left off, and see if she can pass the stick on to me. Maybe she can live out what she didn't get to do through me."

One of Garth's as-yet-unrealized ambitions is to record a duet with his mom. "I'm still looking for the right song," he says. "I haven't found it yet, so I may have to write one."

Both Ray and Colleen had been married before, and the six children had three sets of parents between them. But the Brooks clan hung together. Garth was especially close to his brother Kelly, who is a year older and his only sibling to share both Ray and Colleen as biological parents.

"I raised my family to love God, their family, and their country, in that order," Colleen has said. "Garth follows that to this day, and I'm very proud of the way he's turned out. He knows what's real, and it gives him an anchor. That's why I'm not afraid of how he's going to deal with all this attention. He's good, solid people."

In 1977, as a freshman at Yukon High School

One family tradition was Funny Night, in which everyone took turns entertaining the others by telling jokes and stories, each trying to top the last. As the baby of the family, Garth usually came out a winner.

Garth has described growing up in the Brooks household as "like a weekly sitcom on TV. It was *fun*. Our house was a place where we could be kids—it wasn't some place that was always kept immaculate where we

That same year, Garth was elected Vice President of his ninth grade class. He poses here with other officers.

couldn't touch anything or do anything. We could do anything we wanted to as long as we didn't tear the house down.''

That may have been how it felt on the inside, but it looked a little different from the outside. Todd Johnson, who grew up across the street from Garth and went to school with him from second grade through high school, remembers Ray and Colleen as strict disciplinarians. The younger Brooks kids weren't allowed to leave the front yard after school.

"I don't know how many hours me and my brother spent playing football in that front yard with Garth and Kelly," said Johnson. "Garth and Kelly were really close. They used to stage boxing matches in the front yard. One time Kelly got beat, and Garth couldn't fight after that, it tore him up so much.''

Johnson remembers Garth as basically a typical small town kid who rarely got in any trouble worse than accidentally throwing a ball through a window. "Garth was just Garth," he said. "He was kinda nutty. He liked to goof off and he liked attention, but it was never anything extraordinary. I never expected anything like this. I remember the first time I saw him on TNN. They were doing a show on the new country stars and I thought, 'God, he's as good as the rest of those guys!' "

Johnson's family owns the Yukon Trophy shop on Main Street, where tourists can purchase souvenir Garth Brooks Blvd. signs and miniature Garth Brooks water towers. He shakes his head at the extremes to which some fans will go to get close to a star. Johnson says that before Ray and Colleen moved to their new spread near Edmond on the other side of Oklahoma City, they had to contend with people knocking on their door day and night looking for Garth.

"We have people come through here, and they would die for him," he said. "You know what bothers me? These people feed their kids on Garth. I guess if there's anyone you should idolize, it's Garth. But what if he does something and lets 'em all down? These kids are going to be destroyed.''

But, like most of Garth's old childhood friends and neighbors, Johnson is proud and happy for Yukon's favorite homeboy. "A few people maybe feel a little bit of jealousy, because of all the money he's making," he said. "But I think ninety-nine percent of the people here say it couldn't have happened to a nicer guy.''

GARTH'S WORLD

Ray and Colleen were and are diehard country fans, and there was music going on around the Brooks household all day long. Although she no longer performed in public, Colleen still got out her guitar and led family sing-alongs at backyard barbecues. Ray played a little guitar as well. From a very young age, Garth was soaking up the classic country songs of Hank Williams, Sr., George Jones, Marty Robbins, and Merle Haggard. At the same time, his older brothers exposed him to soft rock and folk singer-songwriters such as James Taylor, Townes Van Zandt, Tom Rush, and Dan Fogelberg. His sister Betsy, nine years his senior, was the first member of the family after Colleen to take music seriously. She was performing Joan Baez and Joni Mitchell songs while still in high school in the late sixties. Betsy later played with Oklahoma country singer Gus Hardin and eventually joined Garth's band as a bassist in 1990.

Garth's own adolescent tastes tended toward hard rock, although he seems to have gravitated to the sound and image of the music without identifying too strongly with rock's underlying rebellious impulses. Like many kids of his generation, his favorite band in junior high school was Kiss, while his high school playlist included mainstream rock radio acts such as Elton John, Billy Joel, Fleetwood Mac, Boston, Journey, and Kansas. Yukon isn't exactly "Wayne's World" territory, and Garth was no stoner, but it's not all that difficult to picture him bouncing around in a car with his high school buddies singing along with Queen's "Bohemian Rhapsody" like a "Saturday Night Live" skit.

All of these elements—the traditional hard-country roots, the romantic pop-folk lyrics, the rock energy and showmanship—would be recycled and turn up in new forms on Garth's albums and in his live concerts. The mainstream rock of the seventies is viewed with disdain by most critics and the post-punk generation, but Garth is not ashamed to admit how much he liked artists such as Boston, Elton John, and Billy Joel. In fact, he *still* likes them. He taught himself to play piano so he could perform Elton's "Candle in the Wind" and told *Rolling Stone* that he upholds Boston's first album as the ideal guitar sound for his own albums.

"I'd just like to see the lyrics of the Taylors and Fogelbergs matched with the music of the Joneses and Straits."

20

And every country fan knows what Garth did for Joel's "Shameless" when he took a forgotten pop album track and refashioned it as a huge country hit.

Perhaps the most impressive aspect of Garth's artistry is that he's technically surpassed most of his influences—at least those from the pop side. He's reshaped his diverse musical inspirations from the sixties, seventies, and eighties into a country sound that's obviously right for the nineties. In virtually every interview he gives, Garth credits country stalwarts George Jones and George Strait as his vocal role models and soft-rockers James Taylor and Dan Fogelberg as his favorite songwriters. "I'd just like to see the lyrics of the Taylors and Fogelbergs matched with the music of the Joneses and Straits," he told me.

But back when he was absorbing all these styles in junior high and high school, few who knew Garth thought he was serious about music—probably because he wasn't. Sure, he plunked around on the banjo and guitar, sang in the school chorus, and formed a high school garage-rock band called The Nyle. But Garth's first passion was sports. He played football and baseball in high school and dreamed of a career as a professional athlete. (Some dreams die hard. In his 1992 tour book, Garth admits that one of his unfulfilled fantasies is to play third base in a major league baseball game.)

"He wasn't one of those kids that you get so danged tired of that's always pulling out their guitar and singing in the halls," said Huckaba, whose son used to ride to and from school with Garth. "If you were gonna predict something like this about a kid, I don't think it would have been this kid."

Nor would anyone have predicted athletic stardom for this kid. Although he played quarterback in football and outfield and pitcher in baseball, Garth was hardly a candidate for the high school All-America team. Major colleges weren't beating down his door with scholarship offers.

Garth now looks back and laughs at his athletic endeavors. When the *Yukon Review* referred to him as a high school football star on his last homecoming visit, Garth noted that "star" wasn't exactly the right word to describe his performance. "If you've really done your homework, you know I didn't star," he said. "I pretty much sucked on the gridiron. As a quarterback for the Yukon Millers, we went 0–5, so I'm not too proud of that."

Larry LoBaugh, who coached Garth in his junior year, said the coaches decided to try him at quarterback his senior year because of his strong arm and leadership potential. Garth's problems, according to LoBaugh, resulted from a lack of foot speed and an unfortunate tendency to throw the ball to the other team. "He wasn't supposed to be a quarterback," said LoBaugh, who recently retired as principal at Yukon High. "But we didn't have a very good team that year and he was all we had."

After the coaches moved a junior to starting quarterback in the sixth game of the season, Garth returned to his previous positions—defensive lineman and tight end. LoBaugh said Garth accepted the change calmly, and the team rebounded from its disastrous start and almost made the play-offs.

Steve Lowry

Proud parents Ray and Colleen Brooks

"He was a pretty tough kid," LoBaugh said. "I think he played as hard as he could all the time."

But Todd Johnson, who played linebacker on the team, said Garth might have been hurting inside more than the coaches were willing to acknowledge. His older brothers all had been outstanding players, and Garth may have felt he was letting his family down as well as the team.

"I think he had a hard time dealing with failure," Johnson said. "There was one game in particular we lost that we should have won. He . . . well, he just had a hard time dealing with it. He didn't get mad. He turned inward."

In the late seventies, Yukon High's student body basically was divided into four sociological subsets. You had your jocks, your preppies, your cowboys, and your stoners. Although the groups sometimes overlapped, Garth was recognized as a jock. He usually wore tennis shoes and ball caps, not boots and cowboy hats. He grew his hair over his ears on the sides and almost down to his shoulders in the back.

In 1978, a high school sophomore

But Johnson said Garth didn't hang out that much with the other jocks. "He was always a part of everything, but he never really hung out with the crowd. He wasn't much of a partyer. After the games, he usually just went home."

Looking back, Johnson feels Garth's religious beliefs might have determined his behavior more than he and the other kids realized at the time. "From my observation of Garth growing up, he was a pretty conservative guy. He had strong family values. He didn't drink. I don't remember him going to church much, but his mom told me he always had a strong belief."

However real, this belief didn't preclude Garth from going out with girls. "He loved the girls," LoBaugh said. "He always had lots of girlfriends."

Garth once described himself to *People* magazine as "pretty much of a dick" during his high school days. "Had to be the center of attention. Went from one girl to another. I was pretty shallow," was his analysis of himself as a teenager.

Yet, he also did things most jocks wouldn't do. In twelfth grade he tried out for and won a leading role in a school play. An average or above-average student in most subjects, he excelled in English and writing. Even his coaches noticed his flair for language. "He was kind of a poet," observed Huckaba. "He was always writing poems and giving them to girls."

One girlfriend, described as his high school sweetheart, eventually grew tired of Garth's romantic fantasies and told him that she wanted to go out with a real man—someone living in the present instead of always dreaming about the future. That girl (who has asked to remain nameless) later became the inspiration for Garth's song "Unanswered Prayers," in which a married man runs into his old high school flame at a football game and finally realizes how much better off he is with the girl he's got.

Garth says the song is "word for word autobiographical, except [the meeting] wasn't at a football game. It was at a crafts fair."

In 1979, as a junior at Yukon High, Garth ran for Yearbook King with Ginger Godwin as his prospective Queen. They lost. We wonder what she's doin' now.

That same year

Garth briefly considered joining the Marines upon graduating from high school in 1980. But Ray, the ex-Marine, had other ideas. All the Brooks children had gone to college and enrolled in career-oriented programs, and Garth was not going to be the exception.

Most of the kids in Yukon root for Oklahoma University in the intrastate rivalry with Oklahoma State. But when it comes time to pick a college, many kids choose OSU in Stillwater. It's far enough away (about a ninety-minute drive) to establish a measure of personal independence from the folks, yet it's close enough to come home for Sunday dinner.

Garth had his own reasons for picking OSU. His brother Kelly, a championship hurdler in high school, had gone there the year before on a track scholarship. Kelly encouraged Garth to come up and try out for the team. Although his high school athletic achievements had been less than spectacular, Garth still longed to compete in sports. At just over six feet tall and about two hundred pounds, he was too small to play on the line in college football and he didn't foresee much of a future for himself as a quarterback. He might have tried out for the baseball team, but Kelly suggested another, perhaps more realistic, option: throwing the javelin.

This Greek-inspired Olympic event didn't exist at Yukon or other Oklahoma high schools, so few athletes at OSU had any more experience at chucking the spear than Garth. While he was too slow to be a sprinter and too small to throw the discus or shot put, he'd always had a powerful arm and exceptionally strong legs. In the javelin toss, he found an event in which his in-between size was an asset rather than a liability. Garth made the team as a freshman walk-on candidate and was one of two javelin throwers awarded a partial scholarship in his sophomore year.

"After a couple of years of catching it, they allow you to throw it," Garth is fond of telling people who ask about the javelin. He's also been quoted as saying, "If they'd have had a good coach for the javelin, I wouldn't have had the scholarship."

The outdoor track season is in the spring, but the training goes on year round. Garth embarked on a serious weight-lifting program. He put on about twenty pounds of muscle, and eventually could bench-press nearly three hundred fifty pounds. (Or, as one writer put it, "The combined body weights of Randy Travis and Dwight Yoakam.") After the regular track and field events are completed at a meet, it's customary for the weight throwers to race, just for fun. With his stocky build, Garth reportedly was a terror in this unofficial event, known as "the fat man's relay."

One of Garth's regular workout partners on the team was Dale Pierce, a shot-putter and discus hurler. The two have remained friends—Pierce sang in the chorus on "Friends in Low Places"—although he says Garth's incredibly busy schedule makes it difficult for them to keep in touch these days.

"Garth is in the top three of the most dynamic people I've ever met in my life," said Pierce, who has a carpet-cleaning business in Stillwater. "Even when he's down, he's up. Personality just oozes out of him."

In 1980, during halftime at a football game, Garth poses for pictures with Yukon High's Homecoming Queen Jerri Castro. What a difference a year makes.

Unlike most people who knew him before he went to Nashville, Pierce says he is not surprised by his friend's success. "Garth is a very determined person," Pierce declares. "When he sets his mind on something, he does it."

Pierce believes Garth draws his strength from a higher power. "He has a gift from God. It's a unique quality. He understands what talent is, and where it comes from."

A bluegrass lover, Pierce plays guitar and dobro. He and Jim Kelley, a graduate assistant with the track team who also played guitar, liked to pick a little bluegrass and country in the dorm or on the bus. When Garth joined the team the following year, he sometimes accompanied them on banjo and guitar. "That was the most fun part of my life," says Pierce. "It made the road trips seem a lot shorter."

Those fans who've seen Garth drop to his knees and pound the stage while singing "Shameless" might wonder if this unabashed emotionalism has a basis in real life or if it's strictly showbiz. Pierce has no doubt that it's real. He'll never forget Garth's reaction when they learned that Kelley, a former athlete who was popular with many of the students, had been killed in a plane crash. "There was a solid wood door," Pierce said. "He hit that door with his fist as hard as he could and broke his hand."

Garth dedicated his first album to the "loving memories" of Jim Kelley and Heidi Miller, another college friend who died in an auto accident.

But such intense emotional reactions apparently were not typical of Garth during his college years. Jim Bolding, OSU's track coach in the early eighties, recalls him as "a real easygoing, fun-loving kinda guy. He was well liked by his team members and certainly was never any trouble at all."

Bolding says he still hasn't figured how Garth managed to balance his schedule between traveling with the team, keeping up with his studies, working a part-time job, playing music, and maintaining some kind of social life. "He never had any trouble sleeping on the bus," Bolding noted. This ability no doubt has served him well many times since.

Jeff Fair, OSU's athletic trainer, remembers Garth as a healthy specimen who didn't require much special attention from the medical department. If

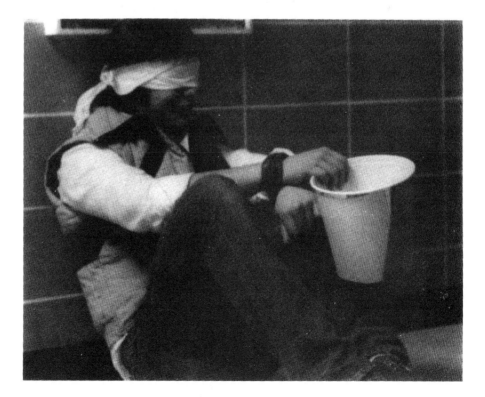

Garth was "kidnapped" before a football game by Yukon High pranksters. Here he attempts to raise money for his "ransom."

Garth goes over some plays with Yukon High's football coach Milt Bassett, 1980.

he had it do over again, however, Fair might have treated Garth with a little more respect.

"I used to kid around a lot with the kids," Fair said with a chuckle. "Not too long ago, this trainer I know in Montana called me to say he took care of a former patient of mine. I said, 'Who?' He said, 'Garth Brooks.' I guess Garth was on tour and was having some trouble with tendinitis in his knees. So the guy asked Garth if he knew me. He said he did, and that I had called him a pussy one time. It just shows you got to be careful who you're callin' a pussy. He might wind up a multimillionaire."

Through sheer determination more than abundant natural ability, Garth developed into a competitive javelin thrower in the Big Eight conference. He was hardly a contender for the U.S. Olympic team, but he did make it to the conference finals in his sophomore and junior years with a personal best of about 210 feet.

After he failed to make the cut in the qualifying round in his senior year, Garth recalls lying in the high-jump pit at the University of Nebraska. As he tells the story now, he was feeling thoroughly dejected, and was bitterly facing the realization that his days as an competitive athlete were coming to an end, when a coach walked by and told him, "Well, now you can get on with what matters in life."

"I wondered," says Garth, "what the hell could *that* be?"

As a high school senior, 1980

WELCOME TO WILD WILD WILLIE'S

"It hit me one day that this is what I want to be doing for the rest of my life."

Garth might not have known for sure what he was going to do with his life, but by this time he knew what he *wanted* to do, and that was make music.

Garth has said he had an opportunity to go to Nashville to work at Opryland U.S.A., the theme park built around the Grand Ole Opry, prior to his senior year at OSU. His parents insisted that he stay in Stillwater and finish school. "So I made a deal with them that I would finish and they would morally support me in whatever decision I made," Garth told a reporter in 1990.

In December 1984, Garth graduated from Oklahoma State with a degree in advertising. He has described himself as an indifferent student. "I did what I needed to do to get by, and if I could do one thing about college, I would listen to my dad more and study harder," he has said.

Some of Garth's friends speculate that the reason he chose advertising as a major was to further his understanding of how to market himself in the music business. "I thought [music] was all he wanted to do, all he cared about," says Mike Platt, who threw the javelin with Garth at OSU and worked with him as a bouncer at the Tumbleweeds country dance hall.

As might be expected of a college town, Stillwater has a far more active music community than most towns its size. The strip of live music clubs and bars on Washington Street near the campus resembles a smaller version of Austin, Texas, long recognized as a musical hotbed. Indeed, Stillwater has been called "the Austin of Oklahoma." In the mid-eighties, a listener could hear live music coming out of several bars within a few blocks of each other. Stillwater even has its own homegrown sound—an organic blend of folk, rock, country, and blues known as "red dirt music."

Before he began working professionally as a musician, Garth liked to take his guitar to the Student Union and serenade the students for free. He landed his first paying gig at a pizza parlor when he was nineteen and soon was sitting in with bands and working as a solo act in local clubs. Garth met older Stillwater songwriters such as Bob Childers and Greg Jacobs and incorporated a few of their songs into his repertoire. He also began in earnest to try writing songs of his own.

Garth respected Childers and the other Stillwater songwriters, but he never really fit in with their "red dirt" sound. Several of the hipper local musicians hung out at an old house west of town called the Farm, where they would trade ideas for songs and pick around on guitars. By contrast, most of Garth's closest friends were jocks and other students. From the beginning, his musical instincts were more commercial than what was being created out at the Farm. He played primarily for average folks like those he knew back in Yukon, not other musicians and songwriters.

Which is not to say that Garth's music is overly calculated—by Nashville's formulaic standards he's a certified risk-taker. But he seems to have a natural gift for appealing to a broad common denominator. "I think that most of my songs are straight from the heart," he once told the *Orlando Sentinel*. "If you go from the heart, you don't need any rules. People talk about hooks and things like that, but there are no rules for songwriters. It just has to appeal to the heart, and that's kind of all you need. I'm just an average guy, and if it appeals to me, it kind of appeals to the average [person]."

In 1981, Garth heard an album that he says completely changed his outlook on country music. The album was George Strait's *Strait Country*, which featured Strait's first hit, "Unwound," an old-fashioned C&W drinking song with a clever lyrical twist.

By the time he got to high school, Garth by and large had turned his back on his country roots in favor of rock and folk music. The slick country-pop of the seventies had left him cold; it wasn't good country and it wasn't good pop. Strait—a handsome cowboy from South Texas—was singing pure country-western music in the tradition of Bob Wills, George Jones, and Merle Haggard, like what Garth's parents had played at home when he was a kid. But he was doing it with a stylish flair and a consistent sense of taste that younger listeners like Garth could relate to. Meanwhile, pop music in the early eighties was moving away from the folk-flavored, lyric-oriented styles he'd admired in the seventies toward MTV's postmodern mix of new wave, metal, and rap. Garth became, in his own words, "a George wanna-be."

In 1990, when his band opened for Strait's Ace in the Hole Band for the first time at a concert in Jackson, Mississippi, Garth told a reporter he was scared to death. "George Strait is a very huge hero and an idol of mine—and for all the members of my band," he said. "He's no hype. Strait held on to real country music during the urban cowboy days. He's solid-colored shirts and a white hat, you know."

When Garth was voted male vocalist of the year in 1991 by the Academy of Country Music, he thanked "Mr. Strait" for showing him the way, declaring, "He'll always be *my* male vocalist of the year."

Yet, when Garth approached owners Bill and Dolly Bloodworth of Willie's Saloon in Stillwater for a gig the following year, he didn't know any of

Strait's songs. His repertoire consisted almost entirely of acoustic pop and folk covers.

"This kid just wandered into the bar one day," said Dolly. "He said, 'I'd like to audition.' I said, 'I don't usually take auditions, but go ahead.' He leaned against a pool table and played a few tunes. I thought he had a good voice, so I figured 'Why not?' "

Dolly says she encouraged Garth to add more country to his act. "When we hired him, my brother came down the first night he played here and asked to hear 'Bandy the Rodeo Clown' by Moe Bandy," she recalled. "He said he didn't know any country-western tunes. When he came back the next week, he knew that song and several other country songs."

Garth played his first night at Willie's for tips. He returned nearly every Wednesday for three years, gradually developing a repertoire of some 350 songs by everyone from Bob Dylan to Slim Whitman. His standard introduction was "Welcome to wild wild Willie's on a wild, wild Wednesday!" He drew a different crowd than most of the other acts who played at Willie's. There were fewer college-rock punks and longhairs, more cowboy hats. Garth himself was usually attired in jeans or sweatpants, an OSU Cowboys T-shirt, and his ever-present ball cap.

A tape of Garth performing at Willie's reveals that he was beginning to combine his country, folk, and pop influences into an original style. Accompanied by his friend Clem Clemons on lead guitar, he did Merle Haggard's "Silver Wings" and Charlie Daniels's "Longhaired Country Boy" next to

"You're standin' on my blue suede shoes, son." Garth meets Carl Perkins.

Steve Lowry

Ball one!

Major leaguer

Foul ball, down the right field line

Elton John's "That's Why They Call It the Blues," Dave Loggins's "Please Come to Boston," and Dylan's "Don't Think Twice." His voice sounded much as it does now; sweet and smooth, but with enough of a cowboy yodel to give even the most saccharin pop songs a definite taste of red dirt country.

Garth also specialized in musical impersonations. "He could imitate anybody," says Dolly. "He did that 'Highwayman' song, and he did all four parts—Willie, Waylon, Johnny Cash, and Kris Kristofferson. When he did start to do his own tunes, he called them his 'worthless originals.'"

Although some of the musicians and songwriters out at the Farm scoffed at his act, Garth gradually built quite a local following. He had his own fan club in Stillwater long before he went to Nashville. He also traveled as an entertainer with The Posse Club, an OSU alumni fundraising organization.

"He met a lot of people that way," Dale Pierce said. "Wherever Garth went, he spread a lot of goodwill. Everyone who heard him sing knew he would be successful at it. What they loved about him was that he did other people's songs better than they did. People would walk up to him and ask him, 'What's your name? I want to buy your first album when it comes out.'"

Others recall the situation rather differently. Unbelievable as it might seem to those fans who waited in line for days trying to get tickets for the 1992 tour, going to see Garth at Willie's on a Wednesday was no big deal for some people.

"Back in those days, there was a lot of good music in this town," said Vince Dudenhoeffer, general manager of Tumbleweeds. "It wasn't like, 'Hey, let's go see Garth!' It was more like background music. He was just another guy up there with a guitar. Who would have thought he'd come back and be bigger than God?"

At some point during this period, Garth must have realized that music was his true calling. He made a commitment to himself to pursue it as far as he could. "One day I realized I was doing this six nights a week and practicing three to four days a week," he explained to yet another interviewer. "I thought to myself, 'Well, maybe this might be what I need to be doing here.' It hit me one day that this is what I want to be doing for the rest of my life."

While Garth was gaining a reputation around Stillwater as a talent to watch, he still wasn't making enough money to support himself at music. He took a job working weekends as a bouncer at Tumbleweeds, which is where he got in the habit of wearing a cowboy hat to work. It's also where he met the woman who would become his wife.

Tumbleweeds is a typical western dance hall on the outskirts of Stillwater. The club occasionally presents country acts that tour nationally, but most nights a DJ spins current and recent country hits for dancers who waltz and two-step in a circle around the floor. The place caters to students, although only those twenty-one and over are allowed to drink. Not that Garth ever drank much anyway when he and Kelly and Mickey would hang out

Tammie Arroyo / Celebrity Photo

there. He wasn't a total teetotaler, but no one seems to remember ever seeing him drunk.

Garth has said he really wasn't big enough to be a bouncer at Tumbleweeds, which is how he wound up with a unique assignment. "All the men in Oklahoma are either five-four and square or six-ten and weigh about four hundred pounds," he said. "So they made me handle all the disputes involving women."

Mike Platt, Garth's buddy from the track team who worked with him at Tumbleweeds, laughs at this explanation. "It's true that there were other bouncers bigger than Garth, but he was probably more interested in messing with the girls than he was breaking up fights between guys," Platt said. "But if there was a fight, he'd be there to help. That's how all the bouncers were."

One night, Garth was called upon to investigate a disturbance in the ladies' room. As he has recounted the story many times, he entered to find a shapely blonde in tight jeans and a cowboy hat with her arm stuck in the pressed plywood wall. A smaller woman was cowering in the corner. "I missed," said the blonde, who might have been a little toasted on tequila.

"I thought, 'Man, this is nuts,' " Garth has said. "But I helped her get her hand free, and as I was taking her outside I just kept thinking about how good lookin' she was. There was something about her that was just tearing me up. I said, 'Look, the policy is that when we throw a woman out we have to make sure she gets home safely.' She agreed, and I was thinking, 'All right!' I told her, 'Why don't you come up to my place and I'll take you home in the morning when you're feeling better.' She just looked up at me with that sweet little face and said, 'Drop dead, asshole.' "

When she met Garth, Sandy Mahl was a nineteen-year-old freshman from the rural Oklahoma town of Owasso, where she had been a high school cheerleader and a summer lifeguard at the city swimming pool. A former rodeo barrel racer, she loved horses—a passion not immediately shared by Garth. Her major in college was child psychology, which might have helped prepare her both for motherhood and sharing living space with a musician's tender ego.

Years later, Sandy told a reporter, "I turned him down. I think that's what caught his eye." But when Garth called her back politely the next day and asked for a date, she accepted. Garth's friends say he had had several women friends in college before he met Sandy, but she was the first one he seemed serious about. He later would describe her as "a little fireball with a fiery temper, but a great woman who's every bit a lady. And she don't take nothing from nobody, 'specially me."

Sandy's friends teased her at first about going out with a jock. "When we were in school, my friends used to say, 'You're dating him? He's not your type,' " she told *USA Weekend* with a giggle. "Now they call me up telling me how great he is, how they love his music. . . . A lot of people look at me and say, 'Why you?' I ask myself that also. My answer is, because I fell in love with a longhaired country boy long ago. I was there when it was, like, how many ways can we figure out to cook potatoes?"

HANK
SR.
IS
DEAD

"I didn't think I'd have to work to break in."

After Garth met Sandy, according to friends, he settled down and stopped chasing women—at least not so obviously. Nevertheless, when Garth left for Nashville in the summer of 1985, he went alone.

"I was a jerk," Garth has said. "When I left I didn't tell her but I wasn't planning on coming back. I didn't think I'd see her again once I moved to Nashville."

Bill and Dolly Bloodworth had put up the money for Garth to cut a demo tape of his songs to take with him. Before he left, they held a big send-off party for him at Willie's. Garth figured he'd go to Nashville and within a few weeks he'd be signed, sealed, and delivered as the next country star. He lasted exactly one day in Music City before running back to Oklahoma with his tail between his legs.

Looking back, Garth says he can't believe how foolish he was. "I didn't think I'd have to work to break in," Garth told UPI correspondent Jim Lewis in 1989. "I came out here really thinking there was nobody as talented as I was. I was really naive. I was twenty-four. I was really a kid at this time. I'm not saying I'm so professional now, but at least I don't have to wear glasses to see where I'm going."

For fifty years, aspiring country singers have been coming to Nashville with the same dreams of stardom that Garth had. Many spend the best years of their lives trying to make the dream come true, only to end up broke, or brokenhearted, or both.

"The only good thing about that trip was that I was not stupid enough to hang around," Garth said. "There was something that kept telling me that this is what I'm supposed to do, but the time sure wasn't right."

When Garth visited Nashville for the first time, country music was at a low ebb. The Urban Cowboy crossover era, launched by the 1980 movie filmed at Gilley's in Texas starring John Travolta and a mechanical bull, had proved to be a short-lived fad. Country radio listenership was down, and even Number 1 records weren't generating enough album sales to be certified gold—the accepted barometer of success in the music

34

business, indicating sales of more than 500,000. The *New York Times*, never a noted critical advocate for country music, had gone so far as to declare the Nashville Sound as ''outdated as the ukelele.''

A handful of young artists such as Strait, Ricky Skaggs, and the Judds were demonstrating that it was possible for country to appeal to younger listeners by cutting through the crossover gloss and glitter and returning the music to its down-home roots while retaining state-of-the-art production values. But most of the Nashville establishment was convinced that the only cure for slumping sales and sagging ratings was more slick, shallow, watered-down country-pop of the sort associated with *Urban Cowboy*. A few years later, after Randy Travis sold more than five million copies of his first two albums, record label talent scouts would be out beating the bushes and turning over rocks looking for young, good-looking guys in cowboy hats who could sing *real* country.

But when Garth pulled into a Holiday Inn near Nashville's Music Row on that rainy day in 1985, Travis was still flipping burgers at the Nashville Palace, Clint Black was still working construction jobs out in Houston, and Alan Jackson was still fixing cars down in Georgia. And country music was in sad shape.

A friend had arranged an interview for Garth with Merlin Littlefield, vice president at ASCAP, one of the two international agencies (the other is BMI) that collects performance royalties on copyrighted songs from radio stations and jukebox owners. Garth was hoping Littlefield might give him some advice or a recommendation to a record company, manager, or song publisher. Instead, he got a cold, hard lesson in reality.

''I sat in Merlin Littlefield's office at ASCAP,'' Garth told UPI's Lewis. ''At the time I left Stillwater, I was making six hundred dollars a week playing clubs. It was not bad money—one hundred dollars a night six nights a week at six different clubs. I got down here and this guy comes in to visit Merlin and Merlin said, 'I'm glad you're finally going to meet a songwriter that's great, an outstanding songwriter.' He was visiting Merlin because he couldn't afford a five hundred dollar loan. That's when it hit me. These guys don't make a million. I told Merlin when the guy went out that I made that much a week. He looked at me and said, 'Go home, then.'

''I walked out of that guy's office hating that guy's guts, *hating* him,'' Garth said. ''And now every day I thank Merlin Littlefield for being straight with me.'' (Littlefield, on the other hand, probably wishes he'd handled the situation somewhat differently, considering what Garth's performance royalties are worth now.)

Asked what he'd learned from his experience, Garth joked, ''That Hank, Sr., was dead. I thought it was a lie.''

On a serious note, he added, ''When you are by yourself for the first time, you really have to prove yourself. You start looking down inside you, about what makes you up, and you start pulling these things out to handle each adversity as it comes. I took a real good look as to who I was for the first time. I was made up of my family, the good Lord, and my friends. None of them were around me.''

As he sat in his hotel room staring at the walls, Garth vowed it would be different when and if he returned to Nashville. ''I came here the first time thinking I didn't need any help,'' he said. ''When I got here I found out I was wrong. The thing about it is it almost takes a death to shake out of it, to realize that God gives you gifts and you use them or you waste them. It took me a trip out here and a very embarrassing twenty-three hours to realize God may have given you the gift but that doesn't mean you can do nothing and get away with it.''

When he got back to Oklahoma, Garth was too embarrassed to return to Stillwater immediately, so he hid out for a couple of weeks at his folks' house in Yukon. His mother later told a reporter from the nearby *El Reno Tribune* that Garth wasn't ready for Nashville the first time he went.

''He had never really been away from home before, had never been alone,'' Colleen said. ''He gets down there and they just shut the door. It wasn't failure. He just didn't know the ins and outs.''

Garth eventually swallowed his pride and went back to Stillwater and to Sandy. He found a day job working at DuPree's Sporting Goods, across the street from Willie's Saloon. DuPree's owner, Eddie Watkins, was a fan of Garth's and tried to accommodate his late-night hours by letting him come in at ten or eleven A.M. If Garth resented waiting on some of the same people in the morning that had clapped for him the night before, Watkins says it didn't show.

''People don't seem to believe, as humble as Garth is, that's how he really is,'' says Watkins. ''What you see is what you get. Everybody says that can't really be Garth. He's too humble, too religious, he gives too much credit to other people. He's not putting on an act. That's Garth.''

Besides selling sporting goods, DuPree's makes custom silk-screened T-shirts for local fraternities and other organizations. In early 1987, when Garth was still a local act dreaming of making it to the big time, Watkins printed up shirts that read ''Garth Brooks World Tour.'' In an example of the loyalty for which he's known, Garth has a contract with DuPree's to make some of the T-shirts he sells on tour, including the *Ropin' the Wind* shirt that reads ''You gotta believe'' on the back.

At night, Garth kept busy playing the Stillwater club circuit. He usually worked as a solo or a duo, but he also liked to sit in with the Skinner Brothers, a classic rock band from Stillwater that played a little country. After the Skinner Brothers broke up in 1986, Garth suggested that they regroup behind him as a country band that played a little classic rock. The band was called Santa Fe, and featured Garth on lead vocals, Tom Skinner on bass and vocals, Mike Skinner on fiddle, Jed Lindsay on guitar, and Matt O'Meilia on drums.

Tom Skinner says that he and his brother initially ''took a lot of shit''

Garth's first foray into the music biz was with a group called Santa Fe. Shown here, left to right: Dale Pierce, Mike Skinner, Garth, Tom Skinner, Matt O'Meilla, Jed Linsay.

from their rock musician friends for playing with Garth. "He picked all the tunes," Skinner said. "We did a few originals, but it was mostly Top 40 country stuff. He'd put on a cowboy hat and sing those George Strait songs with his eyes closed. He really liked that stuff. The rest of us would be back there kinda smirkin'. He wanted us all to wear [cowboy hats], but we couldn't do that."

While Skinner—who sports a thick moustache and a short ponytail—felt somewhat miscast as a commercial country musician, he recognized Garth's charisma onstage. Even when the band was playing at local dance halls and frat parties, Garth would get pumped up before going on. "I always knew he would go somewhere," Skinner said. "Everywhere we went, a certain percentage of the people loved it."

In less than a year, Santa Fe became one of the top-drawing regional bands in Oklahoma, and worked the Southwest circuit from New Mexico to Arkansas. Garth was polishing his act, but he was also learning the downside of being a touring musician. "During that time, I got to learn a lot of the business aspect of music," he told the *Chicago Tribune* in 1989. "I got into a couple of situations where the money wasn't there at the end of the gig, and I had to either fight or get walked on.''

In the spring of 1987, all the members of Santa Fe except O'Meilia decided to move to Nashville. Garth felt he was ready to try it again, and this time he wouldn't be going alone. He had his band, and he had his new wife.

Garth and Sandy were wed in 1986. The ceremony was held in Owasso, where Sandy grew up, and was attended by both families and close friends of the bride and groom. They rented a house near the OSU campus. Although he seemed happy with Sandy, Garth later confessed in *Time* magazine that, at the time, getting married ''was the last thing I wanted to do. I hated being tied down.''

In another interview, Garth said, ''I used to think, when I first got into this business, that Sandy was going to have to start doing everything I wanted her to, or I'd leave her in a minute. I thought, 'All of these women, I can have my choice.' '' Although he frequently gave credit to Sandy for supporting him through the early years of his career, it wasn't until he nearly wrecked his marriage a couple of years later that Garth fully realized how much he loved his wife, and how much she'd contributed to his success by being there for him when he needed her.

The members of Santa Fe rented a big house in Hendersonville, near Nashville. Everyone in the band promised to give it at least six months before anyone quit and went back to Oklahoma or ventured out on their own. But the problems began almost from the day they arrived.

''You stick five guys, two wives, a kid, and a dog and cat in one house, and try and see how you deal with the unknown,'' Garth told the *Tulsa World* just prior to the release of his first album. ''I'm telling you, it's scarier than hell. On top of that, we all had our own different ways of dealing with things, and as a result, everything just kind of fell apart. There were some hard feelings, but not as many as you might think. We're still all interested in what the other ones are doing. We still speak to each other. But it was real scary. Nobody knew what was going on.''

In retrospect, Tom Skinner feels that Santa Fe wasn't the right band for Garth. ''We were not the kind of band a record company would want,'' said Skinner. ''We were all under so much pressure right off the bat. We booked a showcase right after we got there. We sounded *bad*.''

From having lived with Garth, Skinner has a different perspective from those who insist that the real person is every bit as humble and polite as he seems on television and in print interviews. He realizes that his opinion might be perceived as a case of sour grapes, but Skinner claims Garth's regular-guy image is at least partially manufactured.

''He is a real straight guy in a lot of ways,'' Skinner said with no apparent rancor. ''There's a lot of things about him I love. But the image people have of him is phony. For one thing, he's not a cowboy, not that there's anything wrong with that. I remember when Ralph Emory on TNN asked him after 'Much Too Young' came out if he was a real cowboy. I thought,

'This ought to be interesting.' You know what he said? He said, 'I'm not half the cowboy my heroes are.' What a great answer!''

While Garth subsequently has admitted he's never been a rodeo cowboy, he generally comes across as a sincere proponent of traditional American values and decency. But he's gotten a little carried away on occasion, as when he referred to himself in the third person in one 1989 interview. ''I want people to realize that Garth is here for them,'' he declared with all the self-inflated pomposity of a politician on the stump. ''He's here for the American worker, and he's here for the dreamers. 'Cause that's what he is; a guy who believes in workin' for a living, takin' chances and followin' your heart. And that's the kind of people I want to play to.''

In another interview, Garth told a South Bend, Indiana, reporter he was offered a partial scholarship to play football at Notre Dame University but turned it down when OSU offered him a track scholarship. There is no evidence that this is true, and it would seem highly unlikely given his high school football experience. Garth was in South Bend in 1989 to play a free concert in support of legislation that would have made it illegal to burn or abuse the American flag. ''A free concert—that's not much,'' Garth said. ''I don't think it's a right to live in this place. It's a privilege to live in America.''

Skinner contends Garth began to construct his patriotic, All-American persona when the group was still playing bars in Oklahoma. ''He told me before we even went to Nashville he wants to be America's new hero,'' Skinner said. ''He told me, 'America hasn't had a hero since John Wayne.' ''

With Alan Jackson

Laura Luongo / London Features

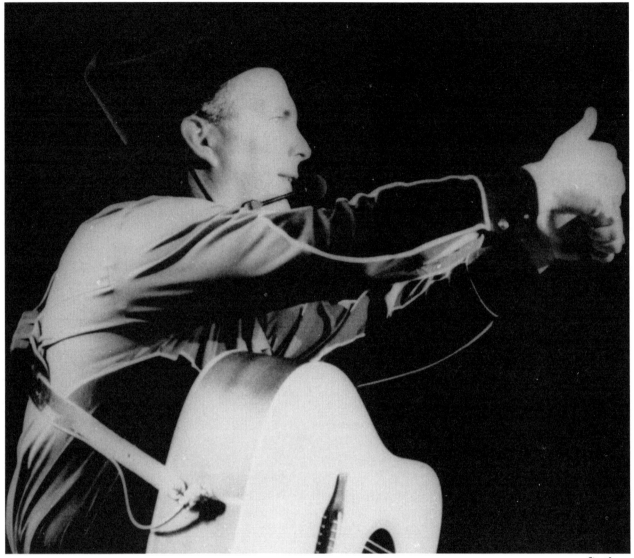

Steve Lowry

After the band broke up, the Skinner brothers returned to Oklahoma. Tom Skinner works for the water department in the city of Bristow, Oklahoma, and Mike Skinner drives a truck. Tom Skinner says his experience with Garth in the band Santa Fe "kinda took the shine off the Nashville mystique. Those [country stars] always seemed bigger than life to me. And I know this guy, who's bigger than life, but I know him in a much smaller way."

Skinner said he hasn't spoken with Garth in a couple of years, but his wife remains on good terms with Sandy. "I can't say enough good stuff about her," Skinner says. "She's easy to talk to, and she always had a smile on her face. She was always really loyal to Garth, too. She really loved the big old corn-fed bastard."

MAJOR
BOB

"Writing is like eating or sex— any time of the day is fine."

Even as his hopes for a record deal with Santa Fe were disintegrating before his eyes, Garth set out on his own to make things happen for himself in Nashville.

The country music business had changed enormously in the two years since he had been there. A long overdue youth movement was in full swing, with labels signing up more new artists than at any time in the history of country music. By the end of the decade, George Strait would be viewed as "the Grand Old Man" of a new generation of stars that includes Reba McEntire, Randy Travis, Vince Gill, Dwight Yoakam, Ricky Van Shelton, Clint Black, Alan Jackson, Travis Tritt, Wynonna Judd, and others. These artists rightly have been credited with bringing country music out of its horrendous commercial and creative slump of the mideighties by reminding young listeners what made the music great in the first place.

For his part, Skinner doesn't blame Garth for the breakup of the band. In fact, he says Garth tried his best to hold the band together for as long as he could and cried when it fell apart. But he suspects Garth also had his own agenda, of which the rest of the band was only dimly aware.

"The guy was smarter than I gave him credit for," Skinner said with a rueful laugh. "I thought you had to work hard and pay your dues and do things right. And he would look me right in the eye and say, 'Tom, you don't have to do that. There's a shortcut to the top of this thing.' That didn't sound right to me. But what do I know? I'm just the water man."

On his first few nights in town, before Sandy and the rest of the band arrived, Garth stayed with Oklahoma songwriter Bob Childers, who had moved to Nashville the previous year. The two had known each other in Stillwater, though not well. Unlike some of the others who hung out at the Farm, Childers had never put Garth down or made fun of him behind his back. But they generally traveled in different circles. Childers is an old hippie who spent the late sixties in Berkeley and settled in Stillwater in the mid-seventies. Garth is a comparatively clean-cut jock from a different musical and cultural generation.

"It may be that he thought I was kind of ornery and wild,"

Steve Lowry

says Childers, who moved back to Oklahoma in 1988. "I thought he was kind of straight."

Like many who knew him when he was just getting started in Stillwater, Childers expresses amazement at how popular Garth has become. But he also says he sensed that Garth had the right stuff to make it in Nashville. "When Garth came down, it was pretty obvious he was going to work," Childers said. "He had the drive and the right attitude. One thing I appreciated about Garth was that he understood how it works in Nashville. You give a little and you take a little. But I didn't figure he'd be *this* big. I would have been nicer to him."

The King of Country

Nevertheless, Childers took it upon himself to show Garth around town and introduce him to some fellow songwriters. One of the first places they went was The Bluebird Cafe, a small restaurant and bar tucked away in a strip mall on Nashville's west side. Although not designed as a music club, the Bluebird has become a creative hub of Nashville's songwriting community. The club is famous for its writers' nights, where four songwriters share the stage, trying out new material and providing vocal harmonies and instrumental accompaniment for each other. Successful writers such as Pat Alger ("Unanswered Prayers," "The Thunder Rolls") and Tony Arata ("The Dance") appear there regularly, and Garth still drops by occasionally to listen for material.

On his first or second night in town, Childers introduced Garth to a songwriter and song publisher named Stephanie Brown. The two hit it off and agreed to try writing together. (Their collaboration eventually produced "Burning Bridges" on *Ropin' the Wind*.)

Brown appreciated Garth's honesty and sincerity, as well as his talent. She suggested he contact an ASCAP executive she knew named Bob Doyle. Garth's previous visit to the ASCAP building, on his first trip to Nashville, had left a bitter taste in his mouth when Merlin Littlefield told him not to give up his day job. But Doyle—a soft-spoken music lover in a business too often controlled by pushy bottom-line types—was impressed by this earnest young singer-songwriter from Oklahoma. Although he was not then in a position to work with Garth directly, Doyle offered to help him find a manager and a publishing contract.

Garth quickly returned to the Bluebird to audition for a spot on a songwriters' showcase. He did a song called "Calm Before the Storm" that has never been recorded. Bluebird owner Amy Kurland still has the scorecard she used to evaluate his potential. She gave him a "4" for the song and a "4-plus" for the performance. She also noted that he was late for the audition. "I've never given a '5' in my life," said Kurland, who has auditioned many of the most talented songwriters in Nashville in the last ten years.

Kurland granted Garth a slot on a writers' night and invited him back several times. She graded a performance of his on March 20, 1988. "He got an A *minus*," Kurland noted with a laugh. "I don't know why I gave him an A minus. I remember being knocked out. He sang a song about putting a woman on a pedestal. I went up onstage and asked him if he'd marry me. The audience loved that."

Kurland recalls that Brooks then looked pretty much as he does now. "Clean shaven, with the hat. He looked like just another writer."

But Garth's fellow writers noticed something different about him right from the start. "I remember the first night I played with him at an Oklahoma writers' night at the Bluebird," says Pat Alger. At the time, Alger was already a successful writer, having penned hits for Kathy Mattea and others. Garth was still another unknown new kid in town.

"We had just written 'Unanswered Prayers,'" Alger continued. "We played the verse and then after we played the chorus the crowd started applauding. That's the only time that's ever happened to me. I knew something was up. He had sort of a *presence*, and he was very serious onstage. I thought he was really talented, but I don't think anybody would have predicted that he'd sell . . . whatever it is now.''

Virtually all of the songs cowritten by Garth on his first three albums were completed before his first album was released. Most observers would agree that Garth's greatest gift is as a performer and interpreter of songs. But his respect for the songwriting process, the pure and difficult act of creation, could be what keeps him honest in evaluating his own talent. Garth has said he misses the camaraderie he felt with other struggling songwriters during this period, before his hectic touring schedule left him with little time to put his ideas down on paper.

''Writing is like eating or sex—any time of the day is fine,'' Garth told freelance music critic Rob Tannenbaum in a story published in *ASCAP in Action* magazine. ''I do it whenever I can. The ideas come twenty-four hours a day. Not that they come that much, but any time, anywhere, the idea'll come to you. If I'm writing by myself, I can pretty much write anywhere. If I'm doing it with somebody, I enjoy sitting around with a couple of guitars, in a room with no windows and no phones, and just beating it out. Often I don't put in that big a percentage of things. Sometimes I just come up with the idea.''

Garth has said he believes the emphasis on lyrics is primarily responsible for country's increasing popularity at a time when so much pop music is focused on videogenic dance acts with little to say to mature, thoughtful listeners. ''Lyricists, that's it, man,'' Garth declares. ''You got three minutes to tell the world somethin', punch right through the chest, grab their heart, and say, *'Listen!'* ''

To illustrate his point, Garth told Tannenbaum about a writer he knows who put his whole life on the line in a song. ''It's about a songwriter who cheated on his wife and really fell in love, but couldn't be with the one he loved,'' Garth explained. ''The whole gist was, while he's writing this song, he knows he's gonna lose his wife, he knows he's gonna lose the respect of everybody, and he'll be alone. But he didn't have a choice, because he's a *writer*.''

It's this heartfelt confessional quality that Garth is seeking in his own songs and in the songs he sings that were written by others. ''That's so cool, when a lyric tears your guts out,'' he exclaims. ''And you say, 'My God, do I want to live this every night?' And you say, 'Hell, yeah, I want to,' because then you know you're living. That's my whole philosophy. My heart's hurting, my soul's hurting, *everything's* hurting. Wow! This is really life.''

But while Garth might look back longingly on his early days in Nashville as a productive period for songwriting, he didn't find being broke and unemployed very much fun at the time. Several managers and publishing companies Doyle spoke to about Garth recognized his talent. But none was prepared to take a chance on a new and unproven client. One successful producer, Barry Beckett, turned him down flat, telling Garth his music had

*P*umping iron

no heart. Meanwhile, his relationship with the other members of the band wasn't getting any better.

One rainy night shortly after he and Sandy moved to Nashville, they were driving home when Garth was overcome by fear and frustration. He had to stop the car because the tears were blocking his vision. He got out in a fire station parking lot and started beating his head on the roof of the car as the rain poured down all around him and Sandy screamed at him to stop. Garth screamed back through the rain and the tears that the situation was hopeless and he couldn't go on.

"I thought we weren't going to make it," Garth told an interviewer. "I thought we were going to crash, trash out, go into debt, poverty, and stuff. It had nothing to do with the music. It was two people, newly married, struggling against debt. I thought it was over."

After they calmed down, he asked Sandy if they shouldn't give up on his dream and go back to Oklahoma. "She sat me down and said, 'Look, I was around when you came back the last time, and I'm not going through that again,' " Garth recounted. "[She said], 'I think you're good enough and you think you're good enough, so we're going to stay right here. We'll get jobs, work, and live here and you'll work on your music.' "

Not long after this episode, the couple were hired as a team by a Nashville store that sold cowboy boots. They worked there for nearly a year. Thanks to his experience working at DuPree's Sporting Goods in Stillwater, Garth became the manager, but Sandy frequently ran the store while he spent his time in the back writing songs.

In November 1987, Doyle left his job at ASCAP to launch his own publishing firm, Major Bob Music. In a remarkable demonstration of faith that has paid off in spades, his first client was Garth Brooks, although Garth stubbornly insisted on waiting until his six-month promise to Santa Fe expired before formally signing anything. Doyle helped Garth find work singing commercial jingles and on songwriter's demo sessions, at which new songs are taped for distribution to prospective singers and producers. That was Garth's voice pitching Lone Star beer and John Deere tractors in 1987 and 1988.

But Garth still needed a manager, someone who knew his or her way around Music City's highly competitive, behind-the-scenes business network. When Doyle was unable to persuade any of Nashville's established management companies to take over Garth's career, he decided to try it himself. While he considered himself a shrewd judge of talent, Doyle realized that his public relations skills were limited. He needed a partner, someone more brash and outgoing than he. He approached Pam Lewis, an independent publicist in Nashville whose clients included young country iconoclasts Lyle Lovett and Steve Earle, about forming a management team.

A transplanted New Yorker with a distinctly noncountry air about her, Lewis had worked at MTV during the music video channel's infancy. She came to Nashville to head the publicity department at RCA Records. After leaving the label, she launched her own PR firm.

"I had been thinking about getting into management, because a lot of people had told me I'd be good at it, and was kind of looking for a partner," Lewis said in an interview at her office. "Interestingly enough, [Doyle] had met Garth and decided to leave ASCAP, and he was looking for a partner, too. He called me one day and we started talking and decided that we'd complement each other well. He said, 'I want you to meet this "boy" I want to work with. I want to manage him and I could use your help. Why don'tcha think about it?'

"So I met this 'boy' he kept talking about, who turned out to be this strapping six-foot guy. He was sitting on this sofa in Bob's office and he had an Alaskan husky dog named Sasha laying at his feet. He stood up and said, 'Ma'am, it's nice to meet you.'

"And it was the most interesting dichotomy of people. Here's this guy from Oklahoma and this New Yorker who started her career at MTV. I was sort of wondering if we'd get along. We talked and I heard him sing and I think we sort of all realized that this could be an interesting marriage with the three of us."

JACK'S TRACKS

"I like to think my lyrics can appeal to . . . everyone from yuppies to rodeo riders."

Doyle/Lewis Management has its offices in an unassuming two-story house on Nashville's Music Row. The house has no sign, and most tourists drive right by without realizing that they've just passed the nerve center of Garth Brooks, Inc. The star himself drops in regularly for meetings when he's in town, sometimes with Sandy or members of his band, sometimes alone.

From the time Garth signed a management deal with Doyle and Lewis in January 1988, his career prospects began to gain momentum rapidly. Doyle introduced him to independent producer/guitarist Jerry Kennedy, who agreed to produce a demo tape of Garth's songs with the goal of landing a major label record contract. Kennedy, in turn, introduced Garth to veteran booking agent Joe Harris of Buddy Lee Attractions, one of Nashville's largest concert tour booking agencies.

Harris, who chased George Strait through several states to sign him to a booking contract when Strait was still an unknown quantity to most of America, quickly became a believer in Garth. He fondly recalls Garth's first visit to his office. "When he sat down with that guitar and sung that first line, I said, 'My Lord!' The first song he played for me was 'The Old Man's Back in Town' [recorded on Garth's Christmas album, *Beyond the Season*]. Every woman in the office came by my door to listen. It was just a gut feeling, that he was gonna be big. He seemed so wholesome. Still, to this day, he tips his hat to the ladies."

Maria Thornton, who now works in the radio promotion department at Polygram Records in Nashville, was a college intern working for Pam Lewis when she met Garth in 1988.

"I can still remember the first time I ever saw him," said Thornton. "He was sitting in Bob Doyle's kitchen, wearing sweatpants, a ball cap, and sneakers, and strumming a guitar. At that moment, I thought, 'Wow, he's gonna be something.' This was before he even had a deal. He had a charisma about him. He's a good singer and a wonderful songwriter, but if I had to pin it down to one thing, he has that *it*."

Even though Garth didn't have a record deal or a touring

band, Harris signed him to Buddy Lee Attractions and began pushing his name to friends and associates in the record business. At Doyle's recommendation, Garth cut back his local club appearances and stopped singing on other songwriters' demos so he wouldn't become overexposed. Still, every label in town passed on Garth the first time around. Some passed twice. The closest Doyle and Lewis had come to a bite was a private audition for Garth at Capitol Records (now Liberty) with former Capitol Nashville chief Jim Fogelsong and former A&R head Lynn Shults. When they didn't hear back from Shults after a few weeks, Doyle and Lewis were prepared to scratch Capitol off their list.

Brian Stein / Star File

Lewis recalls what happened next with obvious relish. "So Garth was scheduled to play a writers' night at the Bluebird—he used to play writers' nights all the time. Lynn Shults came out to see Ralph Murphy, who's a buddy of his. And Ralph, as he is wont to do, was late. So they put this kid Garth Brooks on. Garth was supposed to play at 11:30 on a Tuesday night, and instead they put him on at 8:30. Lynn heard him perform, and said, 'How did we leave this thing?' Garth said, 'Well, you passed on us.' He said, 'Call me tomorrow, we'll talk.'"

Shults, who is now *Billboard* magazine's director of operations in Nashville, remembers the circumstances slightly differently. The writers' night actually was a Nashville Entertainment Association Showcase, and it was Doyle who suggested that Garth fill Murphy's time slot.

"That evening at the Bluebird, he sang 'If Tomorrow Never Comes' and absolutely blew me away," Shults said. "It's what didn't happen [at the audition] in that little room. Garth is an entertainer, not just a recording artist. He feeds on the crowd. When he finished, I went over and told Bob and Garth, 'You guys have got a deal. We'll make a handshake agreement on it right now.' In twenty-five years in this business, that's the only time in my life I did something like that."

According to Lewis, the contract Capitol offered in April 1988 was basically a singles deal, with an option to cut an album later. Garth wanted Kennedy to continue as his producer, but Kennedy was not on good terms with Capitol's management. Shults suggested several other producers, including Allen Reynolds, a respected veteran producer whose biggest hits included Crystal Gayle's "Don't It Make Your Brown Eyes Blue" and Kathy Mattea's "Where've You Been."

Reynolds smiles at the recollection of his first meeting with Garth. "I got a phone call from Bob telling me about this guy he was working with," he explained. "He said, 'I don't know if you're lookin' for anyone or not.' I said, 'I'm not lookin', but I'm open.'"

At the time, Reynolds was producing Kathy Mattea and had a few smaller projects cooking, but there was nothing to prevent him from taking on a new artist. However, he didn't want to waste his time with someone he couldn't get excited about. Reynolds suggested that the three of them—Bob, Garth, and himself—get together for a chat.

"I liked Garth," he said. "He was pretty quiet that first meeting, but he seemed real bright. I thought he knew who he was and what he wanted to do. We liked each other well enough that we decided to do a little bit of work together, just to see how we got along, which is the way I usually do it.''

A few weeks later, when Garth and Allen emerged from the latter's Jack's Tracks studios (built by the legendary producer "Cowboy" Jack Clement), they had cut several tunes that formed the basis of Garth's first album. Capitol was impressed enough with the results that they upgraded Garth's contract to a full album deal. Little more than ten months after he returned to Nashville, Garth had the break he'd been dreaming of for years. Capitol wasn't Lewis's first choice—in fact, she says it was at the bottom of the barrel—but at least they had a real deal with a major label.

Garth initially was concerned that Reynolds might not share his vision, which was to combine George Strait's neotraditional honky-tonk and western swing with sensitive pop-folk ballads. But Reynolds has a reputation for creatively helping artists to develop their own sounds rather than imposing a formula upon them. The two quickly established a working relationship based on mutual respect that continues until this day.

"I give Allen Reynolds a lot of credit for what's happened there," says Waylon Jennings, an old friend of the producer. (Reynolds penned the title track for Jennings's classic *Dreaming My Dreams* LP.) "Garth Brooks didn't get there with his looks. He didn't get there with his personality. And he sure didn't get there with his singing. I don't think Allen ever let him come in there with a bad song and record it. Garth is one of the smarter ones that I've ever seen. But Allen Reynolds gets a lot of credit in my book.''

Reynolds, a modest, soft-spoken sort, shrugs off such praise. "The show is Garth's—it's not my show," he says, sitting in his upstairs office at Jack's Tracks. "I'm always mindful that I'm not the artist. I'm more like a coach. My job is to assist [artists] in presenting their show. I can't work with talent that I don't respect. If I find myself with an artist who doesn't know what they want to do, then I want out.''

Nevertheless, Garth credits Reynolds with offering him a piece of advice that's affected everything he's done since. "It was the first day in the studio and I was bouncing around sounding like a cross between George Strait and Gary Morris," Garth has said. Reynolds stopped him before the session went any further. "Just be yourself," he told Garth. "If you hit, there'll be nobody like you. If not, at least you'll go down true to yourself.''

Garth's first single, "Much Too Young (To Feel This Damn Old)," was released in February 1989. He remembers the first time he heard himself on the radio vividly.

"It's just an amazing feeling that can't be equaled," Garth told the *El Reno Tribune* a few months later. "There's two radio stations in Nashville. I was driving down the road and one of them was playing it. Then I switched stations and it was on there, too. I just wanted to jump out of the truck and yell at everybody, 'Hey, that's me on the radio!'"

"Much Too Young" was the only original song Garth brought with him

Steve Lowry

Steve Lowry

Steve Lowry

Steve Lowry

Steve Lowry

from Stillwater that made it onto his first album. The song originally was about a hard-living musician. He changed it to a saddle bronc rider at the suggestion of Randy Taylor, a friend and cowriter who heard him sing it in a club. The lyrics of "Much Too Young" tell the story of a beat-up and burnt-out cowboy whose life is falling apart while he chases that damned old rodeo from town to town.

Garth managed to work in the name of one of his heroes when he sang, "A worn-out tape of Chris LeDoux, lonely women, and bad booze/Seem to be the only friends I've left at all." LeDoux, a former national bronc-riding champion from Wyoming, is a bona fide western underground phenomenon. Since the seventies, he has been independently releasing and distributing albums of mostly original songs focusing on the cowboy life and the western half of the country-western equation. Garth eventually was able to help LeDoux land a contract with Liberty Records and brought him along as an opening act on his 1991 concert tour. Chris and Garth sing a duet called "Whatcha Gonna Do with a Cowboy" on LeDoux's most recent album.

From the start, Garth announced he wanted to appeal to a broader audience than the stereotypical hardcore country fan. "I don't mind relating my feelings, and I like to think my lyrics can appeal to and be understood by everyone from yuppies to rodeo riders," he said. In one interview, Garth suggested that "Much Too Young" also might describe a cocaine addict, but he added that anybody could relate to the refrain "much too young too feel this damn old."

"Much Too Young" climbed the country singles chart slowly, eventually reaching the Top 10 in July 1989—an encouraging showing for a debut single by an unknown artist. It was not a huge hit, but it served to introduce Garth to country radio audiences prior to the release of his debut album in April 1989.

Produced by Allen Reynolds and engineered by Mark Miller at Jack's Tracks, the album was titled simply *Garth Brooks*. The cover photo pictured a smooth-cheeked Garth staring seriously into the camera. He's wearing a brown felt cowboy hat, a gray Levis jacket, and gray Wranglers, a black and white striped shirt and a white turtleneck. Five of the ten songs were written or cowritten by Garth, including "Not Counting You"—the only track on any of Garth's albums written by him alone. (And, he has said, his least favorite of everything he's recorded, even though the song went to Number 1 when released as a single later in 1989.)

Strait's easygoing Texas swing and new traditionalist honky-tonk influence is immediately apparent on several tracks. "Not Counting You" is a lighthearted western-swing romp. It lacks deep meaning, but it boasts a midtempo backbeat ideal for two-stepping around the floor at Tumbleweeds. The arrangement features spirited playing by fiddler Rob Hajacos, pedal steel guitarist Bruce Bouton, and lead guitarist Chris Leuzinger—key members of the studio band heard on all Garth's albums.

"I've Got a Good Thing Going," cowritten by Garth and Larry Bastian

Ron Wolfson / London Features

with lyrical input from Sandy Brooks, is a bluesy, laid-back country ballad that would fit right in on any of Strait's albums. Garth was proud enough of the song to suggest in Capitol's prerelease press kit that "someone of stature could cut it, like Haggard."

"Nobody Gets Off in This Town," written by Bastian and DeWayne Blackwell, is another swing tune with a clever double-entendre lyric about a tiny town so unappealing that the one stop light is always green and the high school colors are brown. (Garth jokingly has suggested the song refers to Mustang, Oklahoma, Yukon High's arch rival in football.) The track features Garth's loosest vocal on the album—he even yodels a little at the end—and a relaxed guitar solo by Leuzinger.

Bastian also contributed "Cowboy Bill," a traditional western ballad about an old Texas Ranger who entertains the neighborhood kids with stories about life in the wild west. The grown-ups think the old man is just telling tall tales, until they find him dead clutching his badge and "an old yeller letter [that] said 'Texas Is Proud.'"

"Tear my heart out and throw it on the floor, that's what this song does to me," said Garth. "Larry Bastian sat on the couch and played it for me. I asked him to put it on hold for me and he never played it for anyone else."

Another of Garth's favorites was "Alabama Clay," a melodramatic ballad about a young country boy ("his neck was red as Alabama clay") who runs away to the city and then returns to raise his family on the farm. Reynolds suggested "I Know One," a thirty-year-old Jim Reeves classic penned by Jack Clement. Although Garth gives a competent, Patsy Cline–meets–George Strait reading of the song, this is the album's least memorable track.

The most controversial song on the album, at least in the Brooks household, was "Everytime That It Rains." Written by Garth with Ty England and Charlie Stefl, the lyric finds the singer sweetly reminiscing about a one-night stand that took place after hours in a roadside diner. "I'm not going to tell you it's a true story, but I'm not going to tell it's not, either," Garth told country music columnist Jack Hurst. "I love my wife with all my heart, but the woman that song's written about will know when she hears it exactly who wrote it."

In another interview, Garth indicated that Sandy wasn't too pleased when she heard the song. "We've spent a lot of time apart even though we live in the same house because of that song," Garth told the *Atlanta Journal*. "There's nobody else for me but my wife. I wrote 'If Tomorrow Never Comes' for her and it's on the album, too. But there was a life before her that still affects me and my songwriting today. Sometimes it's nice to run back in the playground of my memories."

While *Garth Brooks* received mostly favorable reviews, the new traditionalist honky-tonk slant initially led some critics to mistakenly peg Garth as nothing more than a George Strait clone. Even those who praised him generally did so because they approved of what they perceived as his purist approach to country and western music.

Jack Hurst, writing in the *Chicago Tribune* the week of the album's release, commented, "This is an excellent LP by a newcomer whose talent should enable him to hang around a long time. Offering a fine voice with a strong bent toward the ultra-country side of the spectrum, Brooks' music is more than a little western, as well. His songs combine humor, overpowering emotion and sometimes-steamy sexiness. . . . This is star quality stuff."

Of course, not everyone was equally impressed. John Morthland, writing in the fall 1989 issue of the *Journal of Country Music*, dismissed Garth as "a good example of an artist with potential who is currently in over his head. At 26 he is an inchoate melange of influences—Merle Haggard and George Strait especially—and he doesn't seem to have much grasp of the situations and emotions he sings about, even if he respects them a lot from a distance. . . . For now, he's being carried by his dusty voice alone."

In 20/20 hindsight, *Garth Brooks* rates as an uncommonly solid debut effort. If the album takes fewer chances than Garth's later work, that's to be expected of a new artist. Reynolds's production is superb, emphasizing varied yet restrained arrangements that never overwhelm the vocals. Garth wisely hitched his horses to the new traditionalist bandwagon that was taking over Nashville, and then convincingly demonstrated that he wasn't just paying lip service to the guiding inspirations of George Jones and George Strait.

At the same time, he indicated a willingness to push the limits of traditional country by including contemporary, message-oriented lyrics such as "The Dance" and "If Tomorrow Never Comes." Most reviews barely mentioned these tracks—the two *least* traditionally country tunes on the album. No one, except possibly Garth and Reynolds, predicted that they would turn out to be the most significant for Garth's career.

"If Tomorrow Never Comes" was released as the follow-up single to "Much Too Young" and became Garth's first Number 1 hit. The song combines a gentle country-folk melody with a simple refrain that wouldn't look out of place on a Hallmark card: "So tell that someone that you love just what you're thinking of/If tomorrow never comes."

Yet, just as the corniest Hallmark cliché can induce tears of joy when signed with true love, so does Garth's reading of "If Tomorrow Never Comes" possess an undeniably moving poignancy. Garth has said he got the idea for the song one night while watching his wife sleep and wondering if she would really know how much he loved her if he died. He cowrote the song with Kent Blazy (who wrote "Headin' for a Heartache" for Gary Morris) and dedicated it to his late friends from college, Jim Kelley and Heidi Miller.

"If Tomorrow Never Comes" was evocative enough that Garth said he received a letter from a woman in Virginia who changed her mind about committing suicide after hearing the song. "She was homeless and had a family and she figured they'd be better off with one less mouth to feed," Garth told the *Jackson Clarion-Ledger*. "Then she heard my song just before

Christmas and it changed her mind. Her letter says it isn't easy—they're still struggling—but at least they're struggling.''

Garth told another interviewer the experience had made him more aware of the social responsibility that comes with success. ''Your songs are your swords, your power,'' he said. ''It's amazing the size of the sword you carry. I'm looking for beliefs that need to be stated in this day and time. I try to let people know that they aren't working for nothing, that what they see when they close their eyes at night doesn't always have to be a dream.''

GAME DAY

One of Garth's own most cherished dreams came true the day his album was released. As usual, he described the feeling with an analogy to sports. "All I know is that I'm sitting where I'm sitting with my future in my hands, and that's just the way I like it," he told the *Tulsa World*. "I'm in the big leagues. I'm taking my swings. And it's as fun as it can be."

In any other year, Garth probably would have been considered a leading contender for Rookie of the Year honors. But the same week in April 1989 that Garth's self-titled debut album was released, another good-looking young country singer in a striped shirt and a cowboy hat rode over the horizon into Nashville. The singer's name was Clint Black, and it appeared that he and Garth had more than a few things in common. They were the same age, favored the same style of clothes, and claimed many of the same musical influences. Understandably enough, these striking similarities, combined with the simultaneous release of their debut albums, led to comparisons between the two.

At first, Garth was good-natured about the constant references to Clint whenever his name was mentioned. One poorly edited newspaper in Texas even referred to Garth in print as "Garth Black."

"The similarities between us *are* kinda shocking," Garth told me on his first visit to Houston. "I remember the first time I saw Clint, my wife screamed, 'Come here, I think I'm watching you on TV!' He was wearing the same striped shirt and black hat that I do. His favorite songwriters are James Taylor and Dan Fogelberg. Those are my favorites, too. And he loves George Jones and Merle Haggard. George Jones is king for me. We're three days apart in age. He's from Texas; I'm from Oklahoma. Hell, even my mother probably gets us confused."

But where Garth's first single, "Much Too Young (To Feel This Damn Old)," made a long, slow climb into the Top 10, Black's "A Better Man" rocketed straight to Number 1—the first debut single by a new country artist to reach the top of the chart in fifteen years. And when Garth's debut album was certified gold (indicating sales of five hundred thousand units),

"The competition between Clint and me is the kind that keeps my blood boiling."

Black's *Killin' Time* already had been certified platinum (indicating sales of one million) to become the fastest-selling debut album in country music history.

What's more, Black was something of a critic's darling—not without justification. *Killin' Time* was widely hailed as one of the most important debuts of the eighties, comparable to Randy Travis's *Storms of Life* and Dwight Yoakam's *Guitars, Cadillacs*. By contrast, Garth's debut album received generally good reviews, but few raves.

Although he uncharacteristically bit his lip at the time, Garth later admitted that the constant comparisons with Clint got to him—especially since he kept coming in second. "My debut album wasn't considered by anybody to be a great debut because of Clint Black's album and it was, like, 'Well, there can only be *one* great debut album,'" he said.

That Black's talent justified the hype should have been obvious to anyone who heard *Killin' Time*. But Clint also had a crucial advantage over Garth coming out the chute: He was riding a better horse.

Black was signed to RCA Records, the top-grossing Nashville label through much of the eighties with such high profile acts as Waylon Jennings, Alabama, the Judds, Keith Whitley, and K. T. Oslin. He was managed by Bill Ham, longtime manager of the multiplatinum rock band ZZ Top. By his own estimate, Ham invested one million dollars out of his pocket in start-up funds for Black's career, and RCA took it from there.

As new and relatively unproven managers, Doyle and Lewis couldn't begin to compete with the kind of financial backing provided by Ham, and Capitol's promotion budget was limited. It had been some time since the label had scored a giant money-making hit album.

"We ate Clint Black's dust for a year and a half," is how Pam Lewis describes it. "Our big challenge was trying to establish that while Clint was a very viable act, so was Garth. And while there were some similarities, they were also very different."

The most immediate problem Garth faced was that fans couldn't find his album in the stores. Although Shults insists that Capitol believed in Garth from day one, the label initially shipped only eleven thousand copies of his debut album to retail stores nationwide—not exactly an overwhelming vote of confidence in a product that has sold more than three million since. Lewis says that she and Doyle were so desperate and frustrated at one point that they seriously considered buying advertising on TNN for a 1-800 number so viewers could purchase the album by mail order.

Garth chose to meet the challenge head-on, like the trained athlete that he was. "I've always loved sports," he said. "Without competition, you'll never get any better. That doesn't mean I don't yearn to be number one. It's like when you're in the race, you see the guy ahead of you keep plugging away, trying to eat up ground. The competition between Clint and me is the kind that keeps my blood boiling."

Garth added that while the competition with Clint was real, it wasn't personal. He admitted that he wanted to dislike Clint at first, but found it

"**M**uch too young to feel this damn old . . ."

impossible after meeting him. "I used to think I was the only person in country music whose hero was James Taylor," Garth told *USA Today*. "He and his band are very, very gracious." During one awards show in 1990 in which Clint walked away a big winner, Garth told him backstage, "When you came out, I hated your guts—probably simply because I was envious. . . . But I've grown to love you and what you stand for."

Garth even suggested the possibility of cutting a duet or doing a joint tour with Clint. Eventually, however, the constant comparisons began to wear on him. "I don't mind being called a 'hat act,' because that's part of who I really am and how I dress," Garth told *Performance* magazine. "I don't mind for people to call me a little Strait—I'm a big fan of Strait. It does bother me that some people think that either Clint Black or I will survive, and both of us won't. Some clubs won't play Clint if I'm there, and I hate that they see it that way. I hope Clint stays around forever and I hope I'm here a good while, too."

With the release of *No Fences* in September 1990, Garth finally caught up with Clint. By this time, the stylistic differences between the two had become increasingly apparent. Black is first and foremost a singer-songwriter intent on writing all his own material. He has an immediately recognizable vocal style and a laid-back live presentation. Garth is a more eclectic all-around entertainer who is at his best in front of a rowdy crowd. And while he is a good songwriter, Garth's biggest hits—"The Dance," "Friends in Low Places," "Shameless"—all have been written by others.

Black released his second album, *Put Yourself in My Shoes*, in November 1990. As the two stars battled it out on the charts at the end of the year, the *Los Angeles Times* polled country music insiders on who they expected to sell the most albums in the coming decade. Garth and Clint finished neck-and-neck, well ahead of the rest of the pack. (George Strait was a distant third, while Billy Ray Cyrus was still selling used cars in Los Angeles back then.)

If the same poll were held today, Garth would win in a landslide; he's already ahead of his nearest challenger by about fifteen million albums. Still, it wasn't until *No Fences* demonstrated amazing staying power throughout 1991 that Garth finally distinguished himself from Clint and the rest of the "hat act" pack once and for all.

In a recent article by Robert Oermann titled "How Garth Conquered America: Marketing the New Nashville," Lewis told the *Journal of Country Music* she once turned down an offer from *People* for a cover story on Garth because they would have had to share it with Clint. "At that time there were thirty-five million readers and it was really difficult to turn down," Lewis said. "But we felt we had to make a stand to establish that separate identity for Garth."

Of course, in the first few weeks following the release of his album in the spring of 1989, Garth had no way to know what lay ahead. He was just looking forward to the chance to take his new band out on the road. Capitol had devised a regional marketing strategy based on breaking Garth in the Southwest before promoting him nationwide. He found himself camped out in Capitol's Dallas office and playing the Texas/Oklahoma dance hall circuit—the same circuit that has spawned and supported previous generations of country stars, from Bob Wills and the Texas Playboys, Ray Price's Cherokee Cowboys, and Hank Thompson's Brazos River Boys to George Strait's Ace in the Hole Band.

Steve Lowry

Garth called the band Stillwater, after his musical home. But only one member of the band besides Garth actually had lived in Stillwater—acoustic guitarist and harmony vocalist Ty England. Garth and Ty were roommates for a time at Oklahoma State and had worked as a duet in Stillwater clubs. Garth describes Ty as one of the most "naturally talented" musicians he's known. Garth met lead guitarist James Garver at the Bluebird and renewed the acquaintance when he sold the latter a pair of boots. Garver told Garth he was a fiddler, but Garth suggested he switch to guitar after hearing him play. Garver brought in pedal-steel guitarist Steve McClure and McClure brought in drummer Mike Palmer. David Gant was added on piano and fiddle and Tim Bowers joined on bass. With the exception of Bowers, who was replaced by Garth's sister, Betsy Smittle, this is the same band Garth has today.

Audiences quickly discovered that hearing Garth Brooks on the radio is one thing, seeing him in concert is another. "If you want to hear the album note for note, stay home and listen to it," he warned. "The guys I take out on the road with me are great. We like to have a good time. We stack the [vocal] harmonies, fuzz out the guitars, and turn it up. It's a high-energy show."

Indeed it is. Even when he was still playing clubs and small halls instead of big arenas, Garth brought a virtually unprecedented (for country music) level of energy and theatrical intensity to his live shows. He has said he was inspired by going to see rock bands such as Kiss, Queen, and Kansas when he was in high school. "It was so much *fun*," he said. "I thought, 'Why isn't anyone doing that in country music?'"

When all is said and done, Garth's greatest artistic contribution might be the way in which he's pushed the limits of what is expected, or at least accepted, from country performers in concert. To use one of his own favorite terms, he kicks major ass onstage. He runs around encouraging his musicians, he does a little hip-grinding dance, he pummels the air like a boxer hitting an imaginary punching bag, he giggles uncontrollably, he eggs on the crowd's response by pumping his fist, he untucks his shirt, he swings from a rope ladder at the side of the stage. Next to Garth, those country singers who turn into wooden Indians between tunes come off as old hat, if you'll pardon the expression.

"There is an aura you step in on stage, when the show is going," Brooks told reporter Jill Nelson of *USA Weekend*. "You can see it all over yourself. You get the thumps, where your heart is louder than anything else. Little purple squiggly lines get in your vision and everything starts to look like a negative. And you're just sitting there about to pass out, everything's spinning. It's almost to the point where you can stand there and say, 'Shoot me, watch what happens.' BOOM! Nothing!

"I just want to go up there on that rope ladder, do a triple gainer, land on my head, get up, and just go do it again," he added with a maniacal laugh. "I'm in it for the power!"

Strangely, for a guy who obviously thrives on the spotlight, Garth says

"Lady Luck"

he still gets stage fright before he goes on. "That's the thing that fuels my live shows," he says. "That I care so much about them and get so scared each time out. It's like a catharsis. Each and every concert."

His old friend and road manager Mickey Webber says Garth's intensity onstage comes from athletics. "Once he hits the stage, it's Game Day. He's got a very competitive nature."

Garth admits his enthusiasm has gotten the better of him a few times. He fell off the stage into the orchestra pit at a concert at the Concord Pavilion in California. When he bounced up unhurt, the audience thought it was part of the act.

"When I'm performing in a club and you know everyone is over twenty-one and it's packed wall to wall, this nut comes flying out and it's really interesting to see what he's going to do," Garth told a reporter during his first tour. "Maybe five times in my career he's done something that wasn't that tasteful and we come back and apologize and go on with the show."

Garth declares his main concern has always been to give people a good time for their money. "People are parting with their hard-earned money and time when they come to a show," Brooks has said. "My dad always told me that [the audience] can always get their money back, but they can't get back the time they've spent. The only thing you can replace time with is a memory, so you better make it a good one. . . . They're the ones who put the dinner on the supper table for you."

Before his exploding popularity made it impractical, Garth was known to hang around by the stage after the show for hours signing autographs. Sometimes women would ask him to sign their undergarments, or parts of

Garth and Sandy accept the Lifetime Achievement Award from the Voice of America, March 17, 1992.

Steve Lowry

their bodies. Being the polite sort that he is, Garth usually obliged them. Other women couldn't wait until after the show. They simply pelted him onstage with bras and panties inscribed with messages about what they'd like to do with him if they got hold of him.

Garth professes not to understand why women find him attractive. "Are they blind?" he asks. "There are some superhunks, but I'm not one of them. I'm pale as a sheet. I've got three of these [chins]. I'm losing all my hair up front. . . . If I were a girl, I would be looking for someone more like George Strait. You know, a good-looking man. It's weird, but it's flattering."

But, from the time he began performing in Stillwater, Garth had a way of attracting women fans. He admits he likes to flirt, "to make love with my music in front of women."

In one of the first interviews he gave after the release of his debut album, Garth told columnist Jack Hurst about a night when Sandy was in the audience. "When Sandy gets mad, she counts to herself, and I can usually pick it up at about six or seven," he said. "One night a little girl was drunk and singing on the microphone, trying to get as close to me as she could, and I looked out there and Sandy was on three. I thought, 'Oh, God.' I tried to figure out what to do, but she didn't even get to five. She just stood up, and even though this little gal onstage was pretty good-sized, Sandy grabbed her by the shoulders and threw her off the front of the stage and over the first table."

But Sandy wasn't around to look after her man in those first few heady months with the band on the road. Garth was on his own again, a rising star feeling his oats in the prime of life. He admits the female attention went to his head.

"At first I was on stage and people would bring up drinks and you'd feel like you ought to do something about it, so you'd salute the crowd and nail it," he told an interviewer. "As the night would go on, things got looser. I was losing my voice real bad because I was screaming and just kind of going nuts, staying up all night with the guys."

Garth began to let five or six days go by without calling home, and then he'd act distant when he did. Sandy suspected something was up. An informant on the tour confirmed her worst suspicions. "Garth has always been a very sexual person," she told *People*. "It was his ego, proving he could look out, point, and conquer. What made it easier to cope with was that it wasn't someone special. It didn't mean anything."

Still, it wasn't long before Sandy decided to put her foot down. She called him before a show in November 1989. "I told him my bags were packed, my plane ticket's bought, and I'm gone," she said. When Garth begged her for a chance to explain, she replied, "You come home and we'll talk, on my turf, eye to eye."

Ty England said Garth pretty much lost it during that night's performance. "He was crushed. He choked up during the chorus of 'If Tomorrow Never Comes.' That night changed all our lives. We saw how much we could

Steve Lowry

hurt somebody. Garth has said to me a million times that was probably the best thing that ever happened to him."

It took a long time for Sandy to forgive her husband. "I wanted Garth to feel my pain," she said. "He had hurt me so bad. I had wasted two years of my life, is how I felt. I'd been the perfect little wife who thought everything was hunky-dory. The hardest thing was to keep from beating the holy shit outta Garth at the sight of him. He was ashamed, embarrassed, and it was written all over his face. He broke down like a baby. He was on his knees, more or less beggin' me, 'I'll change, anything. You name it, I'll do it!' "

From that day on, Garth says he started trying to become a better husband. "I wore out a pair of jeans in the knees crawling behind her, trying to get her to stay," he told another interviewer. "Oh, man, I never cried so much in my whole life, never begged so much. The day she told me she would come back is the day I started to become the husband I needed to be."

Not that it comes easy for him. "I enjoy being a husband, I really do," he says. "I suck at it. Have you ever had anything that you really stunk at, but you'd love to try it so much? Well, that's how I am."

He told writer Bob Millard it dawned on him just how much he'd taken his wife for granted when he happened to catch Sandy being interviewed one night on TNN. "Now I was on the outside looking in, and it was a whole different perspective," Garth said. "It had always been difficult for me to be both a singer and a husband, because I always thought they both demanded so much attention and that they were different things. So I just sat there and watched her talk. It wasn't so much what she said, but how she said it. I just watched her mouth move, and for once I was where I couldn't interrupt her and talk over her. I realized this is not just Garth Brooks's wife, this is an individual human being. It gave me a whole new respect for her."

Now, Garth says, the band members—all but one of whom is married— try to prop each other up in weak moments. "When we see somebody falling a little bit, or leanin' it, the guys will get around and just talk to him. They ain't gonna say, 'Don't do this.' They're just going to say, 'Hey, man, you need someone to talk to?' "

At Sandy's request, Garth no longer autographs women's underwear and body parts. "She sat me down, and even though she's a lot younger than me, she told me something about respect. She said, 'They would respect you more if you didn't do that . . . because you are married and you have a commitment to someone not to do that.' "

But Garth admits that temptation is still a problem for him. "To say that we're through the hard times and the storm is over, I think would be very ignorant," he told *USA Weekend*. "Because my music is sexual, it always pushes those buttons. I will have to fight temptation from inside me for the rest of my life, as long as the music is there." He added that the only solution is to "bleed it for all you've got and put it to music. That's a great way to write."

THE FRANCHISE

"I could've missed the pain . . ."

Near the end of 1989, Capitol Records in Nashville underwent a management shake-up. Jim Fogelsong was out as label chief; Jimmy Bowen was in.

Bowen is regarded as something of a visionary by the country music establishment. He broke into the music business in 1956 in Clovis, New Mexico, by releasing a two-sided single with rockabilly legend Buddy Knox. The A-side was Knox's "Party Doll." The B-side was Bowen's "I'm Sticking with You." After his brief career as a teen idol fizzled, Bowen took a job in New York as an A&R man for Morris Levy's Roulette label, which recorded jazz, rhythm and blues, and rock and roll artists. He spent the sixties in Los Angeles, where he worked as a producer at Reprise Records with some of the biggest names in pop, including Frank Sinatra and Dean Martin. Bowen came to Nashville in the early eighties to head the country division at Warner Bros., then jumped to MCA in 1984, where he produced George Strait and Reba McEntire, among others. In 1988 he launched his own label, MCA/Universal, which focused on light jazz and "new acoustic" music.

Bowen likes to portray himself—with some justification—as an outsider who challenged the conventional way of doing things in Nashville. His pop background may have made him more responsive to artists' desire for creative freedom than was customary in Nashville, where a "D.M.C." (domination, manipulation, and control) philosophy too often characterizes a label's relationship with its artists. Perhaps more importantly, Bowen was not afraid to think big. At a time when others in the country music business were desperately worried about hanging on to the shrinking slice of the pie they already had, Bowen foresaw the day when Nashville would challenge New York and Los Angeles as a recording center—not just in country music, but across the musical spectrum.

By the time he left MCA, Bowen no longer could be described accurately as an outsider. He was, in fact, the most powerful man in Nashville. At Capitol he took over an apparently floundering operation that had yet to cash in on the country youth movement of the late eighties. Warner Bros. had

STEVE LOWRY

STEVE LOWRY

Randy Travis and Dwight Yoakam. MCA had Strait, McEntire, Vince Gill, and Patty Loveless. RCA had the Judds and Clint Black. CBS had Ricky Van Shelton and Rodney Crowell. By contrast, Capitol didn't have a current platinum artist on the roster.

When Bowen merged his Universal label with Capitol, he took a hard look at the bottom line. Anne Murray, the label's top-selling artist in the mideighties, was fading, probably because she was too closely identified with the sort of bland country-pop that had fallen out of favor with the new traditionalists. Tanya Tucker remained a viable act, perhaps capable of sustaining the comeback that had begun with her album *Strong Enough to Bend.* Sawyer Brown showed potential, based on the band's popularity as a live act, and Dan Seals had enjoyed consistent radio success. But none of these artists was putting up anything like the kind of sales numbers posted by Travis, Shelton, and Strait.

And then there was this kid Garth Brooks. Garth's debut album had produced two consecutive Number 1 singles in "If Tomorrow Never Comes" and "Not Counting You." But the album wasn't selling especially well given the amount of airplay it had received. Bowen estimates total sales of *Garth Brooks* at around two hundred thousand when he came on board in December 1989.

Opinions vary on precisely how much credit Bowen is due for what happened next. Capitol was planning to release "Nobody Gets Off" as the next single, but Garth pushed hard for "The Dance." He first heard the song when writer Tony Arata sang it at the Bluebird. Arata has said the song was inspired by the movies *It's a Wonderful Life* and *Peggy Sue Got Married* — in which the protagonists are shown how their lives might have turned out differently and come away with the realization that they wouldn't have changed things even if they could. The song's chorus goes, "I could've missed the pain/But I'd have had to miss the dance."

Garth has said he immediately responded to the song's redemptive, life-affirming message. But when Reynolds suggested putting it on the album, Garth reportedly balked. He worried that a semioperatic, string-laden, country-pop ballad would sound out of place next to the more traditional fiddle 'n' steel country tunes on the album.

Reynolds's wisdom prevailed, and "The Dance" became the tenth and last song on Garth's debut album. The arrangement opens with pensive piano and acoustic guitar, then builds to a sweeping climax with a string orchestra coming in behind Garth's impassioned vocal. By the time the album was released, Garth no longer had any doubts about "The Dance." "For me, this sums up the whole LP, my life, and my music," he gushed in Capitol's press kit.

Lynn Shults claims Capitol had decided to release "The Dance" as a single and shot the video before Bowen took over. "We were thinking of going with 'Nobody Gets Off,' but then we said, 'Wait a minute, we've got a serious artist here,' " Shults said. "We had really built a campaign for ['The

Dance']. We felt that's where it had to happen. What we visualized happening happened, but we weren't there."

According to Shults, who was fired from Capitol with Fogelsong, Bowen initially tried to discredit the song. He argued that releasing a fourth single from an album that wasn't putting up big numbers would be like flogging a spent horse. It probably didn't help matters that Garth had auditioned for Bowen when he was at MCA/Universal. Bowen passed, although he now claims he couldn't have signed anyone if he wanted to because his hands were tied by a legal dispute with MCA's corporate headquarters in Los Angeles.

During a break between studio mixes, Bowen said he decided to take a second look at Garth's potential after talking to Allen Reynolds. "He said to me, 'Bowen, you gotta put out the song called "The Dance" and you gotta go see this kid Garth Brooks. He is a *superstar*.'

"I respect Allen Reynolds, and I'd already seen the two hundred thousand sales," Bowen continued. "So I went to see [Garth] work about the second week I'm there. He was opening for the Statler Brothers at a small arena somewhere in Tennessee. That's a pretty old audience, the Statler Brothers. It was awfully gray in there. After fifteen minutes I turned to my wife and I said, 'Oh my God, this is the biggest ever.' This was the third time I'd ever seen that. I saw Elvis do it, I saw the Beatles do it. The kid's eyes were as big as dinner plates. Every eye in the house was on him, but he was on every eye in the house. That's the secret with this kid. He stepped off the stage, picked up a baby, and sang 'If Tomorrow Never Comes.' His natural instincts were incredible. He got a standing ovation from the back of the room to the front. Now, when you get one from the front to the back, everybody has to stand up to see what's happening. This came the other way."

Bowen says he went back to the office and called a meeting of his department heads the next day. "I said, 'We have the *franchise*. Garth Brooks is going to be the biggest that's ever come out of this town.' And they all looked at me like, 'Oh, boy, what happened to you last night?' Even the people who'd been around me a few years knew I was a little crazy, but they'd never heard me say anything like that. Don't forget I had Hank, Jr., Eddie Rabbitt, Reba McEntire, George Strait—some big artists.

"I said, 'Of every dollar you spend, ninety cents better be on Garth Brooks. 'Cause that's our future, and this kid's super.' Every time I hired somebody after that, I made 'em go see Garth."

When Bowen took over Capitol Nashville, Capitol was selling its country compact discs at the midline price. He says he promptly raised the price of Garth's CD to the full price Capitol's pop acts such as Hammer and Bonnie Raitt were selling for. Then he offered the nation's largest record distributors a big discount on the product in lieu of the advertising dollars he didn't have to spend. "I said, 'Put this shit out. Trust me, it's gonna sell.' They did, and it did."

Pam Lewis confirms that Bowen came back a convert after seeing Garth in concert. "He looked at Bob and me and said, 'You *lucky* sons of bitches.' "

Tammie Arroyo / Celebrity Photo

With manager Pam Lewis

Tammie Arroyo / Celebrity Photo

Although the lyrics for "The Dance" imply the death or loss of a loved one, the video featured dramatically lit footage of Garth singing the song spliced with clips of John Kennedy, Martin Luther King, John Wayne, the *Challenger* astronauts, the late country singer Keith Whitley, and the late rodeo champion Lane Frost. Garth and Capitol reportedly fought over the budget for the video, with Garth demanding several edits before he was satisfied.

"If the video can't take a song into a new dimension, I don't want to do it," Garth said. His perfectionist approach paid off when "The Dance" was voted video of the year at the 1990 Country Music Association awards.

"To this day, I think of Garth as a songwriter, and a damn good one," says Arata, who met him back when both were scuffling. "When he listens to songs and picks songs, he does it from the point of view of a songwriter. He was the one who heard 'The Dance' for what it was. The song had been written and pitched around. Fortunately, it wound up at the right time with

Tammie Arroyo / Celebrity Photo

the right person. It received a better treatment than I would ever have imagined. For a songwriter, there can't be a greater compliment.''

"The Dance" became the breakthrough hit Garth and those who work with him were hoping for. In May 1990, *Garth Brooks* was certified gold, indicating sales of more than five hundred thousand. By October, the album was platinum, indicating sales of more than a million. In six months after the release of "The Dance," the album sold five times as many copies as it had in the preceding year. "If Tomorrow Never Comes" and "Not Counting You" had been popular radio hits, but "The Dance" proved to be the kind of major statement that sends listeners into record stores with their money in hand.

Although he's had several other equally big hits, Garth still uses "The Dance" as his set closer, often dedicating it to "a little girl back in Nashville." At the 1992 Fan Fair, where Garth made a triumphant appearance as the once and future king of country music, he told the audience, "This song pretty much wraps up everything I do, whether it goes on forever or it ends this afternoon." And when Troyal Garth Brooks finally is laid to rest in the Friends in Low Places cemetery (which hopefully won't be for a very long time), his epitaph might very well read: "I could've missed the pain/But I'd have had to miss the dance."

RUNNING FREE

"Blame it all on my roots . . ."

For some time, Garth had been promising that his next album would represent a major step forward. In March 1990, before the album was even finished, Garth told a reporter, "What we've got so far for the second album is a turnaround from the first. We have some stuff that went along with the first album that we held off. You should never forget what brought you to the dance in the first place. But they'll definitely see a different side to Garth."

He told *USA Today*, "On the first one I was scared to death to make any kind of mistake. This time we did a lot less intense songs, including one called 'We Bury the Hatchet' [which didn't make the final cut and eventually turned up on *Ropin' the Wind*]. It made the whole session real loose."

Nowhere was that looseness more apparent than on the first single from the album, "Friends in Low Places." Garth heard the song—the tale of a good old boy attending the wedding of an ex-girlfriend who thinks she's too good for him—when he sang on the original demo version for writers Dewayne Blackwell and Bud Lee in early 1989. "I kept hearing it run through my head," he says. "It's the kind of song audiences can sing along to, and that's something I love when I attend a show. So we decided to do it."

But by the time Garth and Reynolds got back around to "Friends," Blackwell had pitched the song to Mark Chesnutt, a young singer from Texas who was working on his debut album. Garth thought he'd had a verbal agreement with Blackwell to hold the song exclusively for him. Both artists wound up cutting the tune—a situation that left neither side happy. It's revealing to compare the two versions. Chesnutt takes a literal approach to the song as a mournful loser's ballad. There's certainly nothing wrong with his vocal—Chesnutt is the best pure country singer to come out of southeast Texas since George Jones—but neither is there anything special about the arrangement to distinguish it from a thousand other sad country songs.

Garth takes the song into an entirely different dimension by turning it into a good-humored declaration of barroom solidarity and class consciousness. From the first lines, "Blame it all on my roots, I showed up in boots," Garth affects an exaggerated, tongue-in-cheek drawl. An informal sing-along chorus—including Sandy, Pam Lewis, Bob Doyle, the members of Stillwater, and whoever else happened to be in the studio at the time—joins in at the end to hammer the point home: Everybody's got friends in low places, and they're the best kind of friends to have. (In concert, Garth never fails to bring the house down by adding a third verse in which the sloshy good old boy tells the snooty ex-girlfriend, "You can kiss my ass.")

"The song tells about who I really am," Garth told an interviewer shortly before its release. "Here I am associating with all these big-name people, but I haven't forgotten where I came from, and who my real friends are. They are the guys back home, just plain old folks, and they are the best people in the world."

Coming on the heels of "The Dance," "Friends" convincingly demonstrated the yin and yang of Garth's artistic range—from unabashed romantic balladeer to unapologetic shit-kicker. The record had to be rushed into release after Garth's mom innocently gave an advance copy to a radio station in Oklahoma City, which immediately threw it on the air and sent taped copies to other affiliated stations. "She doesn't feel too good about it," Brooks said glumly at the time. "The guy who supposedly did it was an old friend of the family. It upsets me to even talk about and give it any more publicity than it's already gotten."

But Lewis viewed the leak as an opportunity, not a problem. Her background at MTV—which boosted the careers of Madonna, Prince, and Boy George, among other controversial artists, in the early eighties—had given her an appreciation for the value of controversy as a marketing concept. "I said, 'We need to exploit this,' " Lewis told the *Journal of Country Music*. " 'When was the last time a country station tried to sneak an album? This is a phenomenon.' So we started a whole media push about the fact that he's so hot people stole the record."

As if according to plan, "Friends in Low Places" made a beeline to the top of the country chart. (Ironically, the Number 2 song during part of its three-week reign at Number 1 was Chesnutt's "Too Cold at Home.") With college students heading back to school in September, the song quickly became a frat-party anthem. Some high school principals objected to students playing the song at school functions on the grounds that it glorifies the use of alcohol as an escape. Without apologizing for exercising his artistic freedom, Garth sided with the principals. "We've had a lot of fun with that song, but it's nothing to base your values on," he told *USA Today*.

No Fences was released in mid-September 1990. Capitol unleashed a full-scale marketing campaign, including television, radio, and print ads and in-store appearances by Garth, who spent the summer on tour as an opening act for fellow Oklahoman Reba McEntire. "There are lots of artists who can sing but who can't impart the emotion and personality that make an entertainer shine," McEntire said. "Garth pulls it off." (Garth subsequently returned the compliment by listing Reba among his favorite singers.)

Capitol's prerelease press kit indicated the extraordinarily high regard in which Garth suddenly was held at the label. "While his music is straight-ahead traditional country, it would be an error to lump this Oklahoma native in with the rest of the pack," read the publicity blurb.

"He is neither just another of the hot new 'hat acts' nor one more in the growing list of crowd-pleasing performers. He's a complex individual, both personally and professionally: A quiet country boy with a deep philosophical temperament and advanced academic degrees; a thoughtful, soulful and emotional vocalist with the capability of turning into a veritable wild man on stage. . . .

"The longevity factor in Garth's career is directly tied to his ability to hear great songs. There's never a throw-away cut on his albums. On the contrary, the gems are often the ones never released as radio singles, but tucked away on the B-side just waiting to be discovered. . . . The disc runs the Garth Brooks gamut from blues to ballad to honky-tonk and back again. No fences, no boundaries, no limit to the man's music."

Of course, the reason record labels have publicity departments is to

A*t Farm Aid, 1990*

Steve Lowry

Garth reaches out to some friends in low places.

Steve Jennings / LGI

make their artists appear to be more talented and interesting than they really are. Experienced reviewers take the hyperventilating prose customarily found in publicity bios with a grain of salt, if they bother to read it at all. That's why they call it hype.

But with *No Fences*, Garth justified many of Capitol's most extravagant claims. No longer could he be accused of merely copying George Strait. With Reynolds's help, Garth had attained the original composite of influences he'd been seeking since his days at Wild Willie's. The album was a tour-de-force of contemporary country styles, from yodeling good-time honky-tonk to sensitive romantic ballads, and from lonesome cowboy fiddle to elaborate orchestrations. Here at last was a commercially successful country artist who wasn't afraid to take chances and buck the assembly-line formulas, even while turning out irresistible, radio-ready smashes like "Friends in Low Places."

Reynolds says Bowen had given him permission to shoot for the moon on Garth's second album. "He said to me, 'Just bring as much of that guy I saw on stage as you can.' Not many label executives would have said that. He felt the energy and in effect said to me, 'Don't hold back. Don't feel like you've gotta be careful and conservative. Let it go.' "

No Fences eventually spawned three more Number 1 singles. "Unanswered Prayers," cowritten with Pat Alger, is a true story based on Garth's bittersweet encounter with his old high school sweetheart. Garth apparently got the idea from Dan Fogelberg's "Same Old Lang Syne," which starts out from a comparable lyrical premise and has a suspiciously similar sounding melody. But Garth takes it a step further when he comes to the mature realization that he's much better off with the woman he's got. "Some of God's greatest gifts are unanswered prayers," he keeps repeating, as if trying to convince himself he really believes it.

"Two of a Kind, Working on a Full House" is Garth at his fun-lovin' finest. "So draw the curtain, honey, turn the lights down low/We'll find some country music on the ray-dee-ay-dee-yo," he yodels. Like others of his suburban baby-boom generation who've made a deliberate choice between country and rock, Garth sometimes comes across as a bit self-conscious when he tries to sing hardcore honky-tonk. As he's the first to admit, he's not a hick from the sticks. But Garth also knows that most of his fans aren't really hicks, either, and so they can relate to his goofy grin when he tips his hat at a rakish angle and sings through his nose in an exaggerated Okie drawl. Buck Owens did the same thing with much the same self-awareness thirty years ago. It's all in good fun.

The fourth Number 1 single from *No Fences* was "The Thunder Rolls," a foreboding tale of a cheating husband who knows he's been caught. With its rock-edged lead guitar and high-tech sound effects, "The Thunder Rolls" was unlike anything else on country radio. In sound and spirit, it has far more in common with the Eagles's "Hotel California" than with Strait's "Unwound"—or, for that matter, with anything on Garth's first album.

As predicted, several of the finest songs on *No Fences* were never re-

leased as singles. "New Way to Fly," cowritten by Garth and Kim Williams, is a brilliantly constructed bar-stool lament boasting a beautiful melody reminiscent of Merle Haggard's "Natural High." (Garth realized his dream of having "someone of stature" cover one of his songs when George Jones recorded "New Way to Fly" in 1992. Garth had the honor of singing harmony vocals with his longtime idol.)

"Victim of the Game," a confessional ballad cowritten by Garth and

At Fan Fair, 1991

Mark Sanders, takes its piano introduction and lyrical cues from Jackson Browne, another of Garth's favorite singer-songwriters. (After he performed at Farm Aid IV in Indianapolis, Garth said, "It was quite a thrill to see myself on the same T-shirt as the great Jackson Browne.")

"Wild Horses"—*not* the Rolling Stones song of the same name—is another chapter in the rodeo cowboy saga that began with "Much Too Young." The arrangement opens with a lonesome fiddle melody played by Rob Hajacos that picks up where the fiddle coda left off on George Strait's "Amarillo by Morning," the prototype of a modern cowboy song.

"Same Old Story," written by Tony Arata, features an understated, yet intensely focused vocal that cuts right to the compassionate heart of the lyric. As McEntire observed, there are plenty of artists who can sing—including some blessed with better voices than Garth's. The difference is that only a handful can be counted on to put a song across when the tape's rolling. Garth usually delivers.

The sleeper cut on the album is "Wolves," a quietly chilling prayer for the survival of the family farm. The last line is, "Oh Lord, keep me from

*P*arty on, Garth!

bein'/The one the wolves pull down." The song was written by Stephanie Davis. "I heard her sing it one night, and it affected me so much I barely remember walking up to the edge of the stage to hear better," Garth said. "I knew right then I had to cut it."

The closest thing to a throwaway track on *No Fences* is a cutesy cover of The Fleetwoods's 1959 saddle-shoe ode to teen angst, "Mr. Blue." The song was written by Dewayne Blackwell, the same Mr. Blackwell who wrote "Friends in Low Places," which might have had something to do with its inclusion here.

Despite his customary aw-shucks humility, Garth couldn't conceal his pride in *No Fences*. "We brought something new to each cut," he said. "In fact, we worked hard to see to it that the record couldn't be labeled and that it wasn't just a remake of my first record. I like running free."

THE MIDAS TOUCH

*N*o *Fences* shipped gold, meaning advance retail orders exceeded five hundred thousand. Within ten days, the album had sold more than seven hundred thousand copies, making it the second-fastest-selling album in the nation, behind only New Kids on the Block. *No Fences* shot to Number 1 on the country chart in its second week, finally knocking Clint Black's *Killin' Time* out of the top spot. It reached Number 12 on the pop chart—the best showing for a country album since Dolly Parton, Linda Ronstadt, and Emmylou Harris went Top 10 with *Trio* in 1988.

By mid-October, five weeks after its release, *No Fences* had sold more than a million copies, certified platinum. (Garth's debut album had gone platinum just the week before.) It seemed as if Garth was accorded a new honor every week. The Country Music Association had nominated him for five awards: male vocalist of the year, single and song of the year (for "If Tomorrow Never Comes"), video of the year (for "The Dance"), and the Horizon Award. The Country Music Foundation in Nashville asked for the brown hat he wore on his first album cover to put on display in the Country Music Hall of Fame. His mother, Colleen Carroll Brooks, donated one of her rhinestone costumes from the fifties at the same time.

Most exciting of all, the Grand Ole Opry invited him to join, making him the sixty-fifth and youngest member to be inducted into country music's most revered institution. Garth has called the night he was inducted the highlight of his career.

"That was *family* there," he told interviewer Celeste Gomes. "That's something I've never, ever accepted, never gotten used to, something I never will. My wife, man, takes to it like a duck to water. She gets to the Opry house, she goes over to Minnie's place, and they sit and they just cackle and laugh, but I can't justify doing that. I just can't understand me sitting there talkin' to Minnie Pearl or Roy Acuff. It's like I don't deserve that. So I just kind of hang out. But Sandy, man, she just loves it. Roy loves her, Minnie loves her, everybody around there loves her, so she feels very much at home there. It's funny, they make me feel very much at home, but at the same time, I don't believe it all sometimes."

"I'd like to thank the good Lord, because He's done a hell of a lot for me."

At the 1990 CMA Awards show, televised from the Grand Ole Opry theater in Nashville, Garth performed a well-received version of "Friends in Low Places." He lost out to Clint Black for male vocalist, Vince Gill for best single, and Kathy Mattea for best song. But he won for best video and the Horizon Award, presented annually to country music's most promising newcomer. (Black had won it the year before.)

Garth's brief acceptance speech for the latter award captured his contradictions perfectly. Like several of the other top male stars at country music's answer to the Grammys and the Oscars, his idea of fancy evening wear consisted of boots, jeans, a tuxedo coat and shirt, and a cowboy hat. He approached the podium, pulling his obviously nervous wife behind him. "I'm not much good at it, but when I don't sing, I try to be a husband," Garth said, introducing Sandy. Then he made a stunningly profound observation. "I'd like to thank the good Lord," he solemnly intoned. "Because He's done a hell of a lot for me."

Although he could see the humor in his turn of phrase, Garth immediately apologized for his gaffe to the press backstage. "I didn't mean to say that," he declared.

In another interview, Garth explained what he really meant. "My peo-

Steve Lowry

Steve Lowry

*G*arth with old pal Ty
England

ple know I couldn't carry a good Christian's shoelaces, but I know all my gifts come from the good Lord," he said. "Our shows talk about values and beliefs and at the same time show you that I'm no saint. I don't think I'm here to preach. I'm here to create music."

The Garth Brooks Express continued to pick up steam through the rest of 1990. By the end of the year, *No Fences* had sold about 2.5 million copies—an astounding figure in such a short time for a country album. "The live shows were catching on, the reviews were great, he was coming into his own, and everything was working to our advantage," said Lewis. "He was like the butterfly emerging from the cocoon. The timing was right."

In March, the Radio and Records readers' poll (comprised mostly of radio and music industry professionals) voted Garth country performer of the year, best male vocalist, best single ("Friends in Low Places"), and best album (*No Fences*). In April, Garth swept the Academy of Country Music awards in Los Angeles. He walked out with an unprecedented six ACM

"Hat" trophies—entertainer of the year, and best single, song, album, video, and male vocalist.

Meanwhile, *No Fences* continued to sell at a phenomenal pace for a country album. In May, *Billboard* changed its method of compiling the Top 200 album sales chart. Instead of asking record store managers to fill out a list numbering their best-selling albums in order, *Billboard* installed a computerized scanning system that tracked actual sales. They discovered what country artists and Nashville business people long had suspected. Many store managers had been underestimating country sales compared to pop and rock—probably a reflection of the historical urban bias against the music. There also were concerns that independent promoters employed by the pop divisions at major labels might have been bribing store managers to make certain albums appear to be selling better than they were.

When the new system went into effect for the May 25, 1991, *Billboard* chart, dozens of country albums showed impressive gains, with Garth leading the charge. *No Fences*, which had slipped down the pop chart out of the Top 20 even while holding firm at Number 1 on the country chart, immediately jumped all the way back to Number 4. This was the highest showing for a country album on the pop chart in ten years.

*G*arth made his TV acting debut on ''Empty Nest'' when he guest starred as himself in an episode titled ''Country Weston.'' He poses here with the cast: Richard Mulligan, David Leisure, Dinah Manoff, Kristy McNichol, and Park Overall.

John Paschal / Celebrity Photo

By May, *No Fences* was well on its way to becoming the best-selling country album of all time. It appeared that Garth could do no wrong. Like King Midas, everything he touched turned to gold. So it came as a shock when the two leading country music video outlets—The Nashville Network and Country Music Television—banned his video for "The Thunder Rolls," citing excessive violence and negative viewer response.

Garth meets with the next generation of fans.

Steve Lowry

Tammie Arroyo / Celebrity Photo

The video for "The Thunder Rolls" depicts a cheating husband (played by Garth in a business suit, wig, and glasses) coming home from a late-night liaison, then beating his wife, who shoots him when he threatens their daughter. The plot is based on a third verse for the song written by Garth and Pat Alger and recorded by Tanya Tucker in 1988, but not heard on the *No Fences* version. Although mild by the standards of MTV and network TV movies, this was hot stuff next to routine country video fare, which typically features footage of the artist lip-synching with a minimal plot line illustrating the lyrics. A guy who got caught cheating might stare repentently at the bubbles in his beer, mourning his lost love, then toss a few pebbles across the surface of his favorite fishing hole. Until Garth, nobody had ever rolled around in the sheets with a lover and beat up his wife. Not on TNN and CMT, anyway.

As *People* put it, the video channels were bothered more by the beatin' than the cheatin'. The controversy arose from Garth's refusal to add a disclaimer at the end of the video. "I did not want to appear to be exploiting the stuff," Garth told me. "If I did the disclaimer, it would have looked like we were trying to make money off abused spouses. I told the networks the disclaimer should be made by someone else. I was reporting real life. That's all I was doing. I take full responsibility for what was in the video. I wouldn't change a thing if I could do it over again."

Needless to add, the controversy worked to Garth's benefit, although Lewis swears she didn't plan it that way. "None of us thought that video would get banned," she said. "We just thought it would be bold. Garth was just trying to make a statement. We had no idea CMT or TNN was going to ban it. We're not that smart. We can't manufacture controversy that way."

Battered women's groups across the nation applauded Garth for helping to publicize an issue few country (or rock) singers have dealt with, at least not sympathetically from a women's point of view. But Garth is still rankled by the ban. "It hasn't hurt my career," he says. "It hurt my feelings. All that work, and then they won't show it. The worst part is, I can't bitch because the same network [TNN] gave me wings with 'The Dance' video."

Garth had the last laugh when "The Thunder Rolls" was voted best video at the 1991 CMA awards. But it's no coincidence that he hasn't released a video since "The Thunder Rolls." (He filmed one for "The River," but chose not to release it. The song went to Number 1 on the country airplay chart anyway.)

"I refuse to make a no-brainer," Garth told *People*. "I would have never, ever [intentionally] done something TNN and CMT couldn't use, but I'm not going to change what I do to fit their standards."

FOR EVERYMAN

"If you let money influence your decisions, then the music will go downhill, because money is the opposite of music."

When an artist becomes as massively successful as Garth did with *No Fences*, he suddenly finds himself dealing with changes in his everyday life he never could have anticipated. Understandably, many are overwhelmed by the experience. It has become a sad cliché in the music business that success changes people, and frequently not for the better. In the most extreme cases—Elvis Presley, Michael Jackson—the stars wind up isolated from reality, living in a fantastic prison of their own creation. But less obvious examples abound throughout the entertainment world. An artist becomes accustomed to celebrity status and gradually forgets where he came from and how he got where he is. Once this occurs, it usually isn't long before the art begins to suffer—especially in a deep-rooted, traditionally minded form such as country music that presumes to speak to and for the common people.

From the time his career took off, Garth has seemed determined not to fall prey to the victim-of-success syndrome. In August 1990, before *No Fences* was even released, he told a reporter he was wary of the way stars receive special treatment. "You're never treated like an everyday person," he groused. "They treat you like a porcelain doll, and all you can do is, don't say nothing and hope you can stay genuine to yourself. When you start believing what they tell you about yourself, you're off the deep end. I have to keep telling myself, 'I'm a kid from Oklahoma and that's all. Just be grateful for this, say your prayers and keep playing with your heart.' "

A few months later, he told writer Bob Millard of *Country Music* magazine he sympathized with what Clint Black was going through after *Killin' Time* made him an overnight sensation. "Unless I'm mistaken, he's a pretty sharp kid," Garth said of his friendly rival. "And that's just what he is, too, man. He's just a kid. They're throwing all this in his face, and he's handling it the best he can." As Millard pointed out, Garth might just as well have been referring to himself.

Garth's old weight-lifting and bluegrass-pickin' buddy Dale Pierce isn't worried about success going to his friend's head. "Garth will never change," Pierce declares. "His faith in God, his friends, and his family won't let him."

Time will tell if Pierce's absolute confidence is justified. But, by most accounts, Garth appears to be handling it remarkably well so far.

"I've seen him tired from the work, but I've never seen him down," says Allen Reynolds, his producer. "I've never met anyone who wore the success so well, and that's the God's truth. I just marvel at him. There's no conflict within him about what he wants to do. I've known other artists who had potential, but there was conflict within them about how much they wanted to give away and how much they were willing to give up of their private lives."

Reynolds adds that the music alone is not responsible for Garth's popularity. "The thing that underwrites Garth is this music that I think so highly of. If it were cheap music, it wouldn't matter to me," Reynolds says. "But it's *Garth* they're responding to. It's *who* he is. This is a guy that would emerge as a leader whether he were in a business setting, a military setting or a political setting. He's a born communicator."

Reynolds believes Garth has the strength of character it takes to preserve a real sense of himself against the onslaught of celebrity. His natural impulse is to be upfront and honest. When the story broke about how Sandy almost left him, Garth told an interviewer he wanted his fans to know the truth. "This is us, this what we do," he said. "We are not perfect, we are just like everyone else, trying to do better."

Garth's manager, Pam Lewis, believes the secret to his success is that people can relate to him. Unlike, say, pop icons Michael Jackson or Madonna, fans find it very easy to imagine themselves in his shoes, or at least hanging out with him. "He's an Everyman," she said. "He's chubby, he's balding, and his grammar's not the best. But he's very human. I've seen him cry onstage."

Still, you get the impression that Garth's humble exterior conceals a healthy ego and a shrewd mind. Not that this is bad. In fact, as Garth concedes, it's probably necessary. "Somebody once told me you've got to have an ego problem to even be in this business," he says. "You've got to have a desire for fame, but at the same time, it's a pulpit to send your message out, to say things that need to be said."

While he freely acknowledges his imperfections, Garth says he wants to be considered a role model for kids. "I feel country music is taking on a new role, taking on responsibility," he said. "We have to consider what we sing, because more and more people are listening to country music, and kids are listening to it earlier. We have the chance to shape society, in a way."

From Merle Haggard's "Okie from Muskogee" to Lee Greenwood's "God Bless the U.S.A.," country music often has been associated with conservative or reactionary political viewpoints. In some of his early interviews, Garth came off sounding like an old-fashioned Republican running for office. "I think we've overshot paradise with a lot of things in life," he once proclaimed. "We need to get the flag back out on the porch and God to the supper table."

When he performed at the Houston Livestock Show and Rodeo during

Steve Lowry

G*arth is mobbed at the 1992 Fan Fair in Nashville.*

the height of the Persian Gulf War in 1991, Garth marched into the Astrodome waving an American flag. The crowd nearly went berserk. But while his patriotism is sincere and deeply felt, Garth says he doesn't consider himself a political conservative. In fact, he says he's never voted for anyone for president because there's never been a candidate he thought would make a difference.

"I'm pretty ignorant on a lot of stuff that goes down, so my opinions are purely based on gut, from-the-heart stuff," he told interviewer Mike Greenblatt of *Modern Screen Yearbook* magazine. "I guess what bothers me most is it seems we're not after what's right but what's most politically expedient, what's Republican or Democrat instead of right or wrong. And that, my friend, is a big batch of bullshit."

Just as Garth's political sympathies are not as clear-cut as at first they might have appeared, so does his personality embrace a fundamental contradiction. An ex-jock and take-charge type, he is unquestionably a man's man. But, at the same time, he's not afraid to expose his deepest, most tender emotions. "He personifies both those sides more than anybody I've known," says Reynolds.

Pat Alger, cowriter of "The Thunder Rolls" and "Unanswered Prayers," calls Garth the most interesting person he's met in twenty years in the music business. "He's a real complex guy," says Alger. "On one level, he seems very simple and down-to-earth. And on another level, he seems very private and sensitive. One thing you find about very famous people as you get to know them: After a while you realize that they're just people. Even Michael Jackson probably has a few close friends who think of him as just a regular guy who loves animals and has strange bathroom habits."

Like others who've worked closely with him, Alger says Garth is very intelligent, more than he's generally been given credit for. "I'll tell you one thing," Alger says. "The guy that's in the driver's seat of his career is *him*. For an artist to genuinely be in charge of his career is very rare in show business. He's the kind of guy who will get up and adjust the lights on the light tower. He knows what he wants. He has a lot of respect for people who do things well, and he certainly does his end of it as well as anyone."

Even Bowen at times has had to yield to Garth's will. "Since I've known him, he's been in charge of everything he does," Bowen says. "The people around him just help him do whatever it is. Garth is not a puppet artist in any respect."

Garth says he has control over everything that his name goes on, and he takes the full blame when things go wrong. But he admits he finds dealing with the business side of his career distasteful. "I don't like the fact that money and sales are put ahead of touching people," he said. "You learn very, very quickly to get people you trust, and get them to take care of it even though you don't. Because if you let money influence your decisions, then the music will go downhill, because money is the opposite of music."

Of course, as an advertising graduate, Garth surely is aware of the importance of image manipulation in marketing. But he's savvy enough to realize that country audiences differ from pop audiences. The latter expect stars to act like stars; the former frown on anyone attempting to get above their raisin'. "It seems like rock people have an image to keep up twenty-four hours a day," Garth says. "With country people, if you've got an image, then you're lying."

Imagine rock heroes Axl Rose of Guns 'N Roses and Bono of U2 taking two or three full days out of their busy touring schedules to do nothing but shake hands with their fans and sign autographs, like Garth does every year at Nashville's Fan Fair. He's sold more albums than any American artist in this decade, yet he still finds time to show his appreciation for his fans. "Garth feels like these are the people that brought him to the party," says Lewis. "Some wait in line for hours to talk to Garth. They're the salt of the earth."

Although he admits it's been difficult at times, Garth says he doesn't believe success has changed him. He's still the same kid from Yukon, Oklahoma, who played football in the front yard and sang "Dirty Old Egg-Suckin' Dog" at the Future Farmers of America banquet. He still wears the same scuffed Roper boots, Wrangler jeans, and Stetson hat he did when he was singing in Stillwater clubs with Santa Fe. His only fashion indulgence is for colorful, collarless Mo' Betta cowboy shirts, handmade by a man named Maury Tate in Apache, Oklahoma.

With Sandy, eight months pregnant, onstage at the 1992 Fan Fair

Garth spent two days signing autographs at the Fan Fair 1992.

E. J. Camp / Outline

Garth credits his father's advice with helping him to keep his feet on the ground. "My dad's always been hovering over my shoulder all my life teaching me things," he says. "He'd say things like, 'Life's a mirror. What happens quickly, goes quickly.' He'd always say stuff like that. My success came pretty damn quickly, and I know it can leave me just as quick. I look at it realistically, and know that tomorrow I could be back to where I first started. But I'll tell you, I'm sure enjoying it now while it's lasting."

SPOKES ON A WHEEL

"No artist is anything without his songs."

Garth attributes the success of *No Fences* to the songs. "I don't care how much hype you have," he told writer Rob Tannenbaum in *ASCAP in Action.* "If your songs aren't there, you're over. No one's gonna have a better *look* than Michael Jackson. No one's gonna have a better *image* than Bruce Springsteen. But that's just part of it, 'cause they got where they are on their songs. And no artist is anything without his songs."

But when Garth and Allen Reynolds got together to discuss plans for his third album, Garth found he had a serious problem. He'd been touring so continuously since the release of his first album that he hadn't had time to write any new material. "I haven't written in two years," he said. "I was out on tour all the time. If you're talking about five minutes to drop everything and put words down on paper, I just didn't have it."

Adding to his distress was the pressure he felt to top *No Fences.* He wanted to prove that the album's huge success was no fluke.

"This one is where the pressure was," Garth confirmed. "If you remember right, my debut album wasn't considered by anybody to be a great album, because of Clint Black's album. Well, now, *No Fences*' object was to stand as a light of its own, but it just shines so much light that it shined light back on the first album. . . . So now I am fortunate to hear people say that my debut album is wonderful as well, but at the time, they weren't saying that, so there really was no pressure on *No Fences* at all."

Garth says that when he went into the studio to start the album, he still didn't know for sure what he wanted to do, but he knew what he *didn't* want to do, and that was to repeat himself.

"Al, my producer, and I sat down, and he said, 'Let's get this thing straight right off the bat; do you wanna make a *No Fences II*?' And he was real quiet. And I said, 'Don't hit me, but no, I don't.' And a big smile came on his face and he said, 'Good. 'Cause there's already one *No Fences*, let's move on.' He said, 'I'm not saying let's move up or move down, but let's just

Steve Lowry

Garth celebrates "The River" going to Number 1 during the summer of 1992.

Steve Lowry

move on and keep taking the chances that we've been taking our whole career.' And I really liked that. It made me feel very, very good about Allen. He keeps surprising me every day.''

Garth also met with Bowen before starting to work on the new album. Bowen recaps their conversation as, ''He said to me, 'Wow, Bowen, I don't know if I can top *No Fences.*' I said, 'Who asked you to? Music isn't about copying oneself. It's about documenting who you are and what you are at that point in time. That's what superstars do.'

''Two weeks later, he turned in *Ropin'*. *Fences* was pretty focused. *Ropin'*, it was like spokes on a wheel. It had half-a-dozen directions, some off to the left and some off to the right. That's the nature of Garth.''

Seven of the ten tracks on *Ropin' the Wind* were cowritten by Garth—more than on either of his previous albums. Although he hadn't written anything in two years, he did have a backlog of tunes he'd worked on before his first album came out. Some, such as ''We Bury the Hatchet,'' had been recorded but not used on the earlier albums. Others, such as ''Papa Loved Mama,'' were unfinished. Reynolds remembers seeing cowriter Kim Williams out in the lobby scribbling down the lyrics to ''Papa Loved Mama'' while Garth was in the studio cutting the other tracks.

''I didn't pick 'em because they were my songs,'' Garth says, almost apologetically. ''These just seemed to be the only ones that fit.''

Unlike those artists who insist on recording only their own songs to maximize their royalties from album sales, Garth felt terrible about using so much of his own material on *Ropin' the Wind*. Reynolds said Garth had a self-imposed quota limiting the number of original songs to no more than half on his earlier albums. He wanted songwriters to feel they could bring their best stuff to him and have a good chance of getting it placed on an album.

''I think outside writers are what has saved me,'' Garth says. ''The two biggest hits I've had, 'The Dance' and 'Friends in Low Places,' were by outside writers. I'm always looking for outside stuff. I really think you get tunnel vision if you have too much of your own stuff on there.''

If, as Bowen suggests, an album should be a documentation of where an artist is at the time, then it's probably significant that the three most memorable originals on *Ropin'* either paint a comic view of marital strife or a melancholy view of the loneliness of life on the road.

''We Bury the Hatchet,'' a jaunty, western-swing tune cowritten with Wade Kimes, might be perceived as Garth's attempts to put his problems with Sandy in the past by joking about them. He seems to take sensual delight in the line, ''Well, I was kissing on Cindy, that I won't deny,'' before adding that it happened a long time ago and it's best to let a dead dog lie. The song's punchline is, ''We bury the hatchet, but leave the handle stickin' out.''

The tables are turned in ''Papa Loved Mama,'' a revved-up country-rocker featuring nasty slide guitar by Chris Leuzinger and slippery fiddle by Rob Hajacos. A truck driver (touring musician?) comes home to find his wife

At the T. J. Martell Foundation Music Row Golf Tournament held at the Hermitage Golf Course in Nashville, September 29, 1991. Here Garth poses with Chet Atkins, Glenn Frey, and Vince Gill

shacked up down at the local motel. "The part she couldn't handle was being alone/I guess she needed more to hold than just a telephone," Garth sings, as if to acknowledge that two can play at the cheatin' game. Perhaps as a good-humored warning, the song ends with Papa ramming his rig into Mama's motel room.

"Cold Shoulder," the album's prettiest ballad, was cowritten with Kim Williams and Kent Blazy (cowriter of "If Tomorrow Never Comes" on Garth's debut album). A truck driver—conceivably the same jealous guy in "Papa Loved Mama"—is stuck in the snow on the side of the highway dreaming of a warm fire, red wine, and soft lips at home. "I wish I could hold her," goes the refrain, "Instead of huggin' this old cold shoulder."

Garth said he got the idea for "Cold Shoulder" when he was driving to Sandy's parents' house for Christmas and saw an eighteen-wheeler parked on the side of the road. Again, the lyric takes on a more personal character if you substitute touring musician for trucker.

Pat Alger collaborated with Garth on "What She's Doing Now." The song is written from the point of view of a guy wondering what his old girlfriend is doing. He finally admits to himself that, whether she knows it or not, "What she's doing now is tearing me apart." The verses add a bit of detail, but the lyric lacks the powerful narrative impact of Alger's previous collaborations with Garth on "The Thunder Rolls" and "Unanswered Prayers," while the string orchestration sounds like someone was trying to make a silk purse out of a sow's ear.

"Burning Bridges" was cowritten with Stephanie Brown, the songwriter who recommended Garth to Bob Doyle right after he moved to Nashville. Garth has said the song is about his younger days, before he met Sandy, and it sounds like the work of a less mature writer. He presents himself as a reluctant womanizer who wants to settle down but always winds up running away: "And I'm always hoping someday I'm gonna stop this running around/But every time the chance comes up another bridge goes down."

The remaining two originals are among Garth's most ambitious recorded efforts. "In Lonesome Dove," cowritten with Cynthia Limbaugh, is a cinematic tale about "a Christian woman in the devil's land" who falls in love with a Texas ranger. It employs all the conventions of a dime-store Western novel, including a climactic shoot-out at the end. Garth has said he tried to come up with another name for the town in which they live. "Obviously, the book and the film had already defined that name," he explained. "But no other title worked as good, so I decided to leave it alone."

"The River," cowritten with Victoria Shaw, is a spiritual testimony with a simple, uplifting message comparable to "The Dance": "So don't you sit upon the shoreline and say you're satisfied/Choose to chance the rapids and dare to dance the tide." It's also the least country-sounding song on the album. The synthesized keyboard, sighing electric guitars, gentle acoustic guitars, and light percussion are straight out of seventies pop-folk, and Garth's vocal plays down the natural twang in his voice.

While some songs are more successful than others, the seven originals

On stage at the 1992 Fan Fair

on *Ropin' the Wind* indicate Garth's increasingly fearless willingness to stretch the boundaries of what is considered country music. Few albums produced in Nashville have displayed a broader range of styles—like spokes on a wheel, as Bowen put it.

But if Garth's originals are the spokes, the three songs he didn't write are the hub that gets the album rolling and holds it together. "Against the Grain," a bluegrass-inflected smoker written for Garth by Bruce Bouton, Larry Cordle, and Carl Jackson, opens the album with a hyperbolic declaration of artistic independence. "Go bustin' in like old John Wayne/Sometimes you got to go against the grain," Garth howls, before turning the hot pickers loose on the tune.

"Rodeo," written by Larry Bastian, is the third chapter in the contemporary cowboy saga that began with "Much Too Young" and continued with "Wild Horses." But where those earlier cowboy anthems employed a traditional western sound, "Rodeo" boasts a funky rock backbeat juiced by keyboardist Bobby Wood's electric piano. The lyrics convey the excitement of

Steve Lowry

America's fastest-growing spectator sport: "Well, it's bulls and blood, it's dust and mud/It's the roar of a Sunday crowd."

At the very heart of the album is "Shameless," an obscure late-eighties album track by Billy Joel refashioned by Garth into a country-rock masterpiece. Garth's vocal comes the closest of any of his recordings to capturing the pound-the-floor excitement of his live shows, while Bruce Bouton's arching pedal-steel guitar lines and Chris Leuzinger's rock-edged lead guitar lend the arrangement a soaring feeling reminiscent of Lynyrd Skynyrd's "Free Bird." Near the end of the tune, Trisha Yearwood enters with some full-throated backup vocals to help Garth bring it home.

Garth has said his first thought when he heard Joel's version of "Shameless" was, " 'My God, why couldn't I have ever said something like that to the woman I love?' There's such great passion in that song, especially if you really look closely at the lyric and what it says. . . . It's like he'll crawl through thirty miles of crushed glass just to get kicked in the face with his lover's boot. And he'll enjoy it! He just loves her so damn much."

Although Garth initially felt that following *No Fences* might be as difficult as "ropin' the wind," he knew he'd given it his best shot. "If I've gotta come to the plate to follow *No Fences*, then *Ropin' the Wind* is the bat I'd grab," he said just prior to the album's release. "It will either be a big loss or a big gain, because it's absolutely not a *No Fences 2*. The way I am wouldn't allow me to try to make a record that was nothing more than a sequel."

WELCOME TO THE NINETIES

"Don't music critics have to graduate from school or something before they let 'em write?"

If *Ropin' the Wind* was not as focused track for track as *No Fences*, you wouldn't have guessed it from the ecstatic public reception. In September 1991, *Ropin'* became the first country album in the history of the *Billboard* sales charts to enter both the pop and country charts at Number 1. At the same time, it became the first country album to top the pop chart in more than ten years. Advance retail orders for *Ropin'* exceeded 1.2 million, and Capitol put together the kind of all-out marketing campaign usually reserved for blockbuster pop releases. Pam Lewis credits Joe Mansfield, former marketing director at Capitol Nashville, with formulating the plan.

"I know Joe discounted the album, got store displays, posters, TV ads, print ads, radio," Lewis told the *Journal of Country Music*. "It was an incredible campaign. He bought up all these ads in blocks, cornered the market so no one else could buy them and basically got all the retail accounts to push the *Ropin' the Wind* album. Joe was the visionary. Bowen said okay and put the money where Mansfield said it should be."

Lewis said that in addition to his public appearances and performances, Garth played an important behind-the-scenes role. "Garth was willing to go to the warehouses, build grass-roots support," she said. "And he continues to do that. Garth has a keen marketing sense. He understands the importance of the people who are loading the trucks, the people shrink-wrapping the product, the truck drivers. He reaches those people and makes them a believer."

But while Mansfield's plan was crucial to the album's fast start, marketing and promotion do not fully explain why *Ropin' the Wind* continued to sell at an average of four hundred thousand copies a week through October. Manfield estimates that Garth's show-stopping performance of "Shameless" on the televised 1991 Country Music Association awards show alone was worth a million in sales.

The two-hour program was hosted by Reba McEntire and featured performances by most of country music's biggest stars, as well as an appearance by President and Mrs. Bush. Garth, who wore a white tuxedo with tails and a white cowboy

Steve Lowry

President and Mrs. Bush pose with participants at the 1991 Country Music Association awards

hat, won four awards, including best album (*No Fences*), best single ("Friends in Low Places"), best video ("The Thunder Rolls"), and the coveted entertainer of the year award. As usual, he dedicated the last award to his heroes, "the Georges," meaning Jones and Strait. He then realized his oversight, and added, "No offense, Mr. President." Ratings for the show, broadcast live from the Grand Ole Opry by CBS, were up 20 percent over the previous year. While the country audience has been growing steadily since the late eighties, the steep increase was mainly attributable to the presence of one man—and it wasn't President Bush.

If many in the pop music industry were surprised by *Ropin'*'s chart-topping debut, they must have been far more shocked to find it still holding the Number 1 spot on the *Billboard* pop chart at the beginning of the new year. Throughout October, November, and December, Garth fended off challenges from some of the biggest names in pop. Guns N' Roses' *Use Your Illusion I*, U2's *Achtung Baby*, and Michael Jackson's *Dangerous* briefly took over the Number 1 spot, as did *Nevermind* by the upstart rock band Nirvana. But after the initial sales rush for each of these albums cooled, *Ropin' the Wind* would reclaim the top spot. Even more remarkably, *No Fences* was still selling almost as well as *Ropin'*. Through late 1991 and well into 1992, Garth frequently had two albums in the pop Top 10 and a virtual lock on the top three spots on the country chart.

In January, NBC aired a special program called "This Is Garth Brooks," consisting mostly of in-concert footage filmed in November at the Reunion Arena in Dallas. At the beginning of the show, Garth appeared in a ball cap and T-shirt to introduce himself. "Hi, I'm Garth Brooks," he said, smiling into the camera. "I'm fortunate to play country music for a living and—wait! I know what you're thinking. Dull!"

As the *New York Times* described it, "The camera cut to a shot of Brooks in concert slamming his guitar into three drum cymbals. 'Old hat!' he said, and the camera showed him spraying streams of water into the air. 'Kinda like watching paint dry.' Two acoustic guitars smashed together, splaying splinters of wood everywhere. 'Well,' he concluded softly, 'all I got to say is, welcome to the nineties.' "

Garth's guitar-smashing routine—a crowd-inciting trick borrowed from the rock band The Who—rubbed some country purists the wrong way. The idea of deliberately destroying a good instrument went against country's hard-working Puritan ethic, not to mention plain old common sense. But younger viewers accustomed to the wild antics of rockers and rappers were enthralled by Garth's high-energy performance, which ended with him

We're Number 1! Jimmy Bowen with Sandy and Garth at a Capitol Records party in Nashville.

Steve Lowry

Steve Lowry

Steve Lowry

"What she's doing now is baking a cake!"

Garth with Pat Alger

swinging from a rope ladder at the side of the stage during a crazy-rocking version of Billy Joel's "You May Be Right."

The same night as Garth's NBC special, CBS aired a special on Michael Jackson. Garth's show drew the highest ratings NBC had enjoyed on a Sunday night in years and was among the ten highest-rated shows of the week. Jackson finished well back in the pack, at Number 66 for the week. As *Rolling Stone* described it, "In an upset that called to mind David and Goliath, a pudgy country singer from Yukon, Oklahoma, had dethroned the King of Pop."

For the first time in the history of American popular music, a guy in a cowboy hat was leading the pop posse. From the earliest country recordings in the 1920s, when the music commonly was referred to as "hillbilly music," country had been considered a secondary market, accounting for no more than 10 percent of total album sales. Country music had rebounded from its mid-eighties slump before Garth came along. But even the best-selling country albums rarely exceeded two million in sales, while a major pop hit by the likes of Michael Jackson or Whitney Houston might sell five or even ten times that much. With the multiplatinum success of *No Fences* and *Ropin' the Wind*, Garth was proving that country could commercially compete with pop without compromising its country identity.

Unlike previous country crossover successes, from Johnny Cash to Kenny Rogers and Dolly Parton, Garth has achieved his across-the-board popularity with minimal airplay on pop radio stations. "Shameless"—which, after all, *was* written by pop star Billy Joel, even if few listeners have ever heard Joel's version—received scattered airplay on pop stations when it was released as a single. But Capitol's pop and country divisions were unable to agree on a plan to work the record at pop radio, and Garth adamantly refused to court the pop market at the expense of his country base.

In November 1991, Bill Catino, vice president of promotion at Capitol Nashville, told *Billboard*, "We'll accept any airplay Top 40 wants to give us. But Garth Brooks has made a commitment here to be loyal to his country audience and to those radio stations. We're getting those listeners to come over [to country radio]. If an artist goes and tries to help them go back the

Country Music Association entertainer of the year, with Sandy

Steve Lowry

Garth with Mrs. Clint Black and Buck Owens at the 26th Annual Academy of Country Music Awards, April 24, 1991

"The good Lord's done a hell of a lot for me."

other way . . . well, his loyalty is to country. At this point, we're not going to help. We're just going to let it happen."

Jimmy Bowen was far more blunt about why he declined to dance to pop radio's tune. "If you want to have a pop hit today, you've got to spend $150,000 on independent promotion," he said. "You gotta spend another $130 to $150,000 on what they call industry tip sheets. You can spend $250,000 to have a pop hit.

"I saw no sense in making that expenditure," Bowen explained. "Why should I go and spend tons of money and make a big effort to reach a younger audience that I see coming to us? It's counterproductive. LA and New York, they still think we're down here waiting for them to call us up. Truth is, we don't give a damn if we ever hear from 'em. We don't want to play their silly game in their silly world. If CHR radio is so controlled by other reasoning as not to add the Number 1 record in America, that's their loss."

In the aftermath of the crossover controversy surrounding "Shameless," Bowen changed the name of Capitol Nashville to Liberty Records to establish a separate and equal identity for his label apart from Capitol's pop division. At the same time, Liberty launched its own alternative rock and pop division to compete with Capitol as well as other pop labels.

For his part, Garth insists he doesn't care if his music is played on pop radio or not. "Hey, man, my music is what I feel on the inside, nothing more," he told interviewer Mike Greenblatt in *Modern Screen Yearbook*. "To tell you the truth, I don't think it even fits on pop radio. And we went out of our way to not push it in that direction at all.

"We're country, plain as day. I feel lucky and also honored to have found a home within country music. And as long as they'll let us stay, that's where we'll go. As far as pop music is concerned, hey, if they play my records, I'll be flattered, but at the same time, if they do decide to play the records I make, they'll know they're playing country records. That's important to me. In contrast to that, I really couldn't care less about pop music."

Even if pop radio continued to ignore the phenomenon of Garth Brooks, other mainstream media did not. Garth's face began showing up on everything from supermarket tabloids and country fanzines to *Forbes*, the respected business magazine. Country music was booming, and Garth was country's most prominent spokesman.

Of course, Garth's massive popularity also produced the inevitable critical backlash. Many pop music critics—especially those based in the media centers of New York and Los Angeles—have tended to regard country music as hopelessly unhip compared to such presumably cutting-edge styles as punk, thrash, metal, and rap. The rise of Nashville's new generation might have caught some critics off-guard and made them uncomfortable about having to risk their reputations covering artists with whom they basically were unfamiliar. Predictably, certain rock critics writing for publications that never before had much use for country music suddenly were born again as country purists. Garth and other young country artists were derided for not

At the TNN Music City News Country Awards held at the Grand Ole Opry, June 10, 1991

remaining true enough to the hard-living honky-tonk tradition of ol' Hank and Lefty.

David Browne, reviewing *Ropin' the Wind* for the *New York Times*, called Garth "the Kevin Costner of country." (Although many American men would take this as a compliment, Browne apparently intended it as a put-down.) The review went on to label Garth "a coffeehouse folkie" masquerading as a country singer before concluding, "For all its Nashville trappings, *Ropin' the Wind* ultimately leaves you with the sense that Mr. Brooks would rather shop at a cowboy boutique than drop by the bar next door."

In a *Time* cover story on "Country's Big Boom" that lumped Garth in

John Paschal / Celebrity Photo

Garth at the taping of the Second Annual Billboard Music Awards, held at the Santa Monica Airport Barker Hangar, December 3, 1991. The program aired on Fox TV on December 9, 1991.

Vinnie Zuffante / Star File

with several other new country acts, Jay Cocks first damned him with faint praise. After calling Garth "part Jolson and part Jagger" and "a hokey holy terror of a performer," Cocks none-too-subtly lowered the boom. "Brooks manufactures a kind of hydrogenated country music—pop and branch water—that has a message and no menace," he wrote. "Just as his live shows have the trappings of rock without rock's edge of danger, or (as in the case of Bruce Springsteen) its all-out emotional engagement."

Garth admitted that the reviews made him mad. "The one thing I have to get used to that I never did before is people taking shots at me more because of *where* I am rather than *who* I am," he told Mike Greenblatt. "It's almost as if to these people the music doesn't really matter anymore. They put me in an awful article with four other 'hat' acts, which immediately made me realize that the people who write these articles about 'hats' and 'boots' don't know shit about country music. They should be writing about something else. They're scared to death that country music's gonna turn out to be something they're gonna have to keep writing about. So they put it down as much as they can in an effort to stop it from flourishing."

Garth told Greenblatt he could accept constructive criticism, but resented being criticized by writers who obviously hadn't been paying attention to the changes in country music. "I remember reading one guy and he was putting me down musically and I was sittin' there goin', 'Yeah, he's right.' But I knew that and I let it go so now I'm payin' for it. Live and learn, man. But these other idiots, wow. Some of 'em really don't have a clue. . . . Don't music critics have to graduate from school or something before they let 'em write?"

Valid or not, the critical sniping ultimately proved to be irrelevant. The public had spoken. Garth Brooks was the biggest musical star in America. By the summer of 1992, Garth had the two best-selling country albums of all time, with *No Fences* at eight million sales and *Ropin' the Wind* at seven million and both still going strong. Meanwhile, Garth's debut album had passed three million in sales and was still in the country Top 10 and the pop Top 40, more than three full years after its release. Sales of the three albums together were closing in on twenty million. No other musical artist in the world could come close to matching this figure in the current decade.

Welcome to the nineties, indeed.

LIFE IS GOOD

In October 1991, Garth announced his intention to take six months off from touring in the first half of 1992. Liberty expected a new album from him every September, and he didn't want to find himself in the same situation as with *Ropin' the Wind*, where he was scrambling for material right up until he went into the studio. Garth and Reynolds also had been assembling a Christmas album for release in 1992.

Garth's goal was to make a few TV appearances, write some new songs with old pals such as Kent Blazy and Pat Alger, and go into the studio fully focused and prepared this time. He also wanted to hang out at home with Sandy as much as possible to rest up and oversee the remodeling of the new house they had bought in Goodlettsville, near Nashville. The home previously was owned by former Nashville mayor Richard Fulton. Garth and Sandy planned to add on to the house's 6,000 square feet and build a roping arena and athletic complex on the twenty-two-acre estate. In the meantime, they moved into a trailer near the house.

Those carefully considered plans received an impassioned jolt the following month, when Sandy learned she was pregnant. In October, Garth and Sandy had snuck off for a quick vacation in Maine before the end of Garth's tour. In the first issue of his new fan magazine *The Believer*, Garth explained that he and Sandy were not really trying to get pregnant—"just practicing," as he put it. In fact, he said, they had agreed to wait another three to five years before starting a family. But Garth claimed he intuitively knew they'd hit bingo at the time of conception. He told Marjie McGraw of *Modern Screen Yearbook* that he jumped out of bed the next morning and took Sandy's picture. When she asked what he was doing, Garth replied, "I want a picture of you the first day you're pregnant." Five weeks later, when her pregnancy test came back positive, Sandy realized Garth had been right on the money.

Garth told reporters about the pregnancy backstage at the Billboard Music Awards, where he picked up another five awards. "I'm speechless, shocked and thrilled," he said. "In about three minutes, I'm taking a flight home. Gonna go up on

"My life has given me some pretty high honors, and even though I'm scared to death, this is by far the highest."

the hill in Nashville to sit with my wife. We just found out we're having a baby. So we are just going to hang out together and be private. . . . This is my first baby. I'm scared. I don't know if I'm ready to be a father, but here it comes!''

Like many expectant mothers, Sandy suffered from severe morning sickness. "For the first eight weeks of pregnancy, Sandy was sick twenty-six hours a day,'' Garth told his fans in *The Believer*. "Finally one night I called her doctor and told the lady that one of us needed some relief. She chose to help Sandy. She guessed I would be all right when Sandy was feeling better.'' But if he had any second thoughts about the pregnancy, Garth kept them to himself. "My life has given me some pretty high honors, and even though I'm scared to death, this is by far the highest,'' he concluded.

Sandy was over the worst of the morning sickness in January, when she and Garth surprised the volunteers at Nashville's Cerebral Palsy Telethon by walking in with a check for $25,000. According to the fan mag *Country Music Superstars*, they'd been watching the show at home and decided to contribute. Later that month, Sandy was feeling well enough to accompany Garth to the American Music Awards in Los Angeles. At the airport in LA, she had what her doctors called a "threatened miscarriage.''

Sandy herself described exactly what happened in the second issue of *The Believer*: "We made the flight fine and were down in baggage claim when all of a sudden without any pain or forewarning I started hemorrhaging. At first we had no idea what exactly was happening, but Garth was great. He rushed me to the ladies' room, left, and called 911. Pam Lewis, his manager, saw us running and came to help. She got first aid while Garth called my doctor in Nashville. Next thing I knew was that we were in an emergency room and the hemorrhaging had stopped. The doctors released me that evening.''

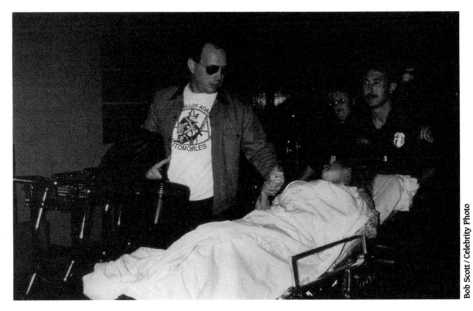

*S*andy is rushed to the hospital after collapsing at LAX due to pregnancy complications, January 26, 1992.

Bob Scott / Celebrity Photo

The next morning Sandy's mom flew out to LA along with Garth's bus driver, Jim Payne. Sandy spent the next three weeks in Tulsa with her mom while Garth returned to Nashville to get the house ready. This occured in the sixteenth week of pregnancy. Her doctors said Sandy had a condition called 'Partial Placenta Previa.' By March 18 the problem had corrected itself.

Partial Placenta Previa is a fairly rare condition where the placenta becomes abnormally situated during pregnancy. Because of Sandy's complications, she underwent seven ultrasound examinations. These examinations allow doctors to determine the sex of the unborn baby, among other medical benefits. After Garth and Sandy were told that they could expect a girl, they decided to name her Taylor Mayne—Taylor for Garth's songwriting hero, James Taylor, and Mayne for the state in which she was conceived. Sandy later added a third name, Pearl, when her friend and Grand Ole Opry confidante Minnie Pearl suffered a crippling stroke.

Needless to mention, Garth never made it to the American Music Awards. He also skipped the Grammys in February, because Sandy had been advised not to fly and he didn't want to go without her. In April, they drove together to the Academy of Country Music awards show in Los Angeles, where Garth repeated as top male vocalist and entertainer of the year.

Sandy experienced no further complications. In early June, she glowed radiantly when she joined Garth on stage at Fan Fair in Nashville, where fans showered them with baby gifts. But between looking after Sandy, television appearances, songwriting and recording sessions, Garth's so-called "time off" had turned into one of the most exhausting periods of his life. He had to hurry to finish both albums before leaving on tour in June. The Christmas album would be called *Beyond the Season*, while his next studio album was tentatively titled *The Chase*. Garth also recorded a duet with his friend and longtime hero Chris LeDoux for the title track of LeDoux's album, *Whatcha Gonna Do with a Cowboy*, and added harmony vocals to tracks by Trisha Yearwood and Martina McBride. Furthermore, the remodeling of his house was taking longer than anticipated, and he was worried that it wouldn't be done by the time the baby was due in July. Sandy wanted the nursery decorated in a Disney motif, with scenes of Mickey and Minnie Mouse on the walls.

"It just about killed me," Garth later told a Salt Lake City reporter of his six-month hiatus from touring. Nevertheless, Garth opened his tour as scheduled on June 2, 1992, in Denver's McNichols Arena, after stopping off in his hometown of Yukon, Oklahoma, on May 31 for "Garth Brooks Appreciation Day." The band, Stillwater, was unchanged except for the addition of acoustic guitarist and backup vocalist Jess Leary, formerly with Reba McEntire's band.

Special writer Butch Hause reviewed the opening night performance for the *Denver Post*. "Brooks's mission was obvious from the start—he intended to outdo past shows, giving the audience even more of the theatrics they'd come to expect," Hause wrote. "A 650-instrument, automated light-

Garth and his mom with Tony and Jaymi Arata at a baby shower for two new arrivals: The Aratas' daughter, Katherine Elizabeth, was born the same week as Taylor Mayne.

Steve Lowry

ing array illuminated a stark, gray stage covered with ramps to accommodate Brooks's mobile antics. . . . With his now familiar headset microphone, Brooks paced the length of the stage like a caged panther, using the ramps to work the audience along the sides and back of the arena. He played little guitar, opting to shake hands and hug members of the audience like a politician. Three songs into the set Brooks told the screaming throng, 'Six and a half months off and it took me one second tonight to figure out that this is where I belong.'"

The concerts sold out everywhere the tour went, frequently in record times. The 16,000-seat Los Angeles Forum sold out in fourteen minutes. In Phoenix, the demand for tickets was so intense the day they went on sale that it knocked the phone lines out of commission for up to an hour around the state and into New Mexico.

At preshow press conferences, Garth said he had no explanation for the exploding magnitude of his popularity. "If I was to pick an individual being recognized as much as me, he would be a lot better looking," he told the *Albuquerque Journal*. "I'm in the dark on this, too." He expressed his disgust at the exorbitant prices scalpers were getting for tickets to the concerts. At Garth's insistence, his concert ticket prices were set at $17, far lower than those for most superstars. Garth wanted his fans to feel they got their money's worth at his shows. It infuriated him that scalpers who paid kids to stand in line overnight to buy tickets as soon as they went on sale could command several hundred bucks a pop from desperate fans. His standard response was, "I've seen the show—it's not worth it. Please don't pay a scalper's price."

H*ome of Garth, Sandy, and Taylor Mayne Pearl Brooks*

John Barrett / Globe

The tour schedule had two weeks open between July 3 and July 17. Stillwater drummer Mike Palmer's wife, Kathy, had become pregnant shortly before Sandy and was due on July 4. Sandy's official due date was July 21, but she and Garth were hoping the stork would come early. "If not," said Garth, "I guess I will have to come home early." In case Garth couldn't make it back to Nashville in time for the delivery, Sandy had a close friend go through Lamaze classes with her and agree to act as her coach.

Garth's timing was impeccable, as usual, with a little help from Sandy's doctors. Sandy gave birth to Taylor Mayne Pearl Brooks shortly before 7 P.M. on July 8, 1992, at Nashville's Baptist Hospital. Taylor weighed seven pounds four ounces and was twenty inches long. Pam Lewis told the *Nashville Tennessean* that "Sandy received no anesthesia, nothing. It was an all-natural birth. Garth was right with her, by her side in the delivery room." Reportedly, Garth's first words were, "After this, nothing else matters." Bob Doyle said he told Garth, "You've had your last full night's sleep." Doyle said Garth replied, "I had my last full night's sleep two years ago."

A week after the birth, Garth met with reporter Robert Oermann of the *Nashville Tennessean* and asked him to relay his thanks to the thousands of fans who had expressed concern and sent so many presents that they had to carry them home in a truck. "All these people deserve to know that the baby and Sandy are fine," Garth told Oermann. "We can't respond to each letter. I just want to thank them . . . If I could sum up life, Sandy, and Taylor in one word, it would be 'perfect.' I've got my girl. Life is good."

Garth added that he was overcome with emotion when faced with the miracle of childbirth. "I feel so stupid," he said. "I'm a man who makes his living putting words on paper and I'm totally speechless. I saw the crown of her head appear and I thought, 'She's gonna be three inches long.' But then this big baby came out. I cut the cord. Then my focus went immediately to Sandy. But Sandy was up on her feet an hour later. I thought, 'My God, how can you do this?' I tell you, my admiration for her has gone up so much."

Garth said Taylor was proving to be a quiet baby. "I was expecting this twenty-four-hour terror. But we only wake up once at night and then at seven in the morning. I'd have another one if it could be a mirror image of this one. But if I had another, it would probably be *me*." He added that he was unsure how the experience of becoming a father would affect his music. "I don't know what I'll get out of this as far as music or songs. Right now I've lost it. I've lost my edge. I'm hoping it will come back."

As Garth had feared, his new house was not ready for the family to live in when the baby arrived. Taylor Mayne Pearl Brooks, daughter of the hottest musical star in America, spent the first few weeks of her life living with her mom and pop in a trailer. Now, *that's* country.

Tammie Arroyo / Celebrity Photo

At a press conference for "Feed the Children," shortly before his performance at the Forum in Los Angeles, July 17, 1992

THE CHASE

"As long as you think the color of skin affects how someone can do their job, as long as you think who someone chooses to sleep with affects how they do their job, it's not a free country, it's an ignorant nation."

Nine days after Taylor was born, Garth was back on the road. And he wasn't the only proud papa in the band; drummer Mike Palmer had a bouncing baby boy waiting for him back in Nashville. But while Garth's stage antics were as wild as ever, inside he was wracked with doubt about his future. His own mother had given up her musical career to raise a family. His parents had always been there for their children when he was growing up. Could he be the kind of father he wanted to be for Taylor and still carry on full-tilt with his career? Garth had been looking forward to his first international tour in 1993. His official tour books were printed in Japanese, Spanish, French, German, and Russian as well as English. As long as he was touring in the United States, it wasn't too difficult for him to fly home to Nashville for a couple of days each week between shows. But that would be impossible overseas, and the thought of leaving Sandy and Taylor at home alone for months was unbearable.

Sandy had made her feelings on the subject clear in an interview with *USA Weekend*. At the time of the interview, Sandy suspected she might be pregnant but hadn't yet taken a home pregnancy test. "He thinks he doesn't give me anything special," she said of her husband. "What he doesn't realize, it's those days when he calls his managers and says, 'OK, today there's nothing,' and takes the whole day to do what I want to do. Those are the days I live for. I see a whole different man than the rest of the United States sees . . . There will come a day in my life when it is just Garth and me. I might be seventy-five and toothless. But that's what keeps me going."

After Taylor's birth, Garth began telling audiences he was confused about his future and hinting that the current tour might be his last. At a news conference before the July 19 concert in Phoenix, Garth declared, "The actual thought of retirement, just getting out for good, is very much in the picture right now because this daughter needs a father, and my wife needs a partner to help raise her. The second that little girl popped out in this world, the one thing that I hit on right away was, 'My

God, all the things that you fought for, that you risked losing friends over, you realize nothing is as important as human life.' "

In late August, Garth appeared at a whirlwind series of press conferences in several cities to promote the release of his Christmas album, *Beyond the Season.* The press conferences were designed as a forum for Garth to announce his joint agreement with Liberty Records and the CEMA distribution network to donate $1 from the sale of each copy of *Beyond the Season* to Feed the Children, the Christian charity based in Oklahoma City. Advance retail orders for the album exceeded 1.4 million, a record for a seasonal holiday album. Garth said he hoped to sell 3 million copies by Christmas, thereby raising $3 million for Feed the Children. He said he also planned to donate an additional sum out of his own pocket.

But questions about Garth's threatened retirement tended to darken the mood and overshadow the other issues at the press conferences. "Right now I'm saying my prayers and talking to my wife and my folks," Garth told the *Los Angeles Daily News.* "I'm asking for the strength to both entertain and be a father. But if I cannot do both, then family always comes first."

He added that if he did continue to tour, it would be because of the fans. "It's been the people that have kept me from quitting, and they're the same people who will keep me from retiring. I don't care for the business that much. It's not the pure, innocent thing it used to be, because it's a multibillion-dollar thing now. Anytime you've got those kinds of numbers, the evil starts weeding in. You've got to deal with the scalpers, the bootleggers, and stuff like that. You go into music thinking it's a pure form that makes you feel good and no one should get in the way of it. Then all you get is people who don't [care] about you or, even worse, don't care about country music. Worst of all, they don't care about your fans. That's like somebody attacking your family."

Reporter Shirley Jinkins of the *Fort Worth Star-Telegram* suggested to Garth that he was sending mixed signals at a press conference at Billy Bob's, the huge country dancehall at the Fort Worth stockyards. "Do you get that from me?" Garth replied. "Well, that's just how it feels to me, too. It's like a punch this way and a punch that way. When I stand onstage I'm so sure that music is what I want to do with my life. But then, offstage, I look at that little girl's face . . . If you focus on something, you've got to give it all you've got. I can't go out there and do music half-assed."

Beyond the Season was released on August 25. While temperatures in Texas and much of the rest of the country were still in the nineties, with humidity to match, here was Garth on the album cover with a dusting of snow on his hat and coat, asking folks to think "beyond the season."

The album features a mix of traditional and nontraditional Christmas songs performed by Garth and his regular studio band, plus guests. Garth is backed by a black gospel choir directed by Donna McElroy on the program opener, the traditional spiritual "Go Tell It on the Mountain." The choir returns, along with a string orchestra, on the closing hymn, "What Child Is This." The original "The Old Man's Back in Town" is in a more traditional

At the 1992 Country Radio Seminar

country vein, and Garth offers an expert impersonation of Buck Owens on the Buckaroos' 1965 vintage "Santa Looked a Lot Like Daddy." "White Christmas" receives an easy-going western-swing treatment, and Garth adds a folksy narration to "Silent Night" about driving home to visit his parents in Oklahoma at Christmas during the first year he and Sandy spent in Nashville. The album's most moving original song is Stephanie Davis's "The Gift," about a poor Mexican girl's humble but pure Christmas offering. Davis and fellow songwriters Pat Alger, Larry Bastian, Victoria Shaw, and Tony Arata—all regular contributors to Garth's repertoire—sing on the traditional children's Christmas classic "The Friendly Beasts."

If *Beyond the Season* sounded good in late August, it promised to sound even better come December. The album entered the *Billboard* Top 200 album chart at Number 4 and rose to Number 2, barred from the top spot only by Billy Ray Cyrus's huge country-pop crossover hit *Some Gave All.* Throughout September, Garth had four albums in the country Top 10—*Beyond the Season, Ropin' the Wind, No Fences,* and *Garth Brooks*—with another blockbuster due out before the end of the month. Meanwhile, the tour rolled on through sold-out dates at Chicago's World Amphitheatre and the New York State Fair in Syracuse, as well as at stops in smaller markets such as Amarillo, Texas, and Springfield, Missouri, and triumphant homecoming concerts in Tulsa and Oklahoma City.

In mid-September, *Forbes* magazine released its annual ranking of the highest-paid entertainers in America. At Number 13, Garth Brooks was the highest-ranking newcomer on the list and the only country artist in the Top 40. *Forbes* estimated that Garth would earn $44 million in 1991 and 1992 combined, right behind Prince's $45 million and just ahead of Arnold Schwarzenegger's $43 million.

Still, Garth continued to ponder his retirement, even as the negotiations on his new recording contract with Liberty continued. His original contract, which called for five albums, would expire with the release of his next album, *The Chase.* Garth told *Billboard*'s Melinda Newman and Edward Morris he had received entreaties from other labels but had no intention of leaving Liberty. "I'm not in this thing to be the highest-paid ballplayer on the field," he said. "I did, however, want to negotiate a deal that stated if I did sell product, I got rewarded, and that's what we've worked out."

But Garth added that the final drafting of the contract had been put on hold until he decided whether to continue as a recording artist. "I feel God put me down here to play music, but it's very evident to see because of the baby, God put me down here to be a father also," he told *Billboard.* "Sandy and I have fifty thousand times more money than we could spend in the rest of our lives . . . The parents, the whole crew, is set up on pension plans, so I can walk away from it. I must decide what I want to do. I think parents work to provide for their children because they have to, and if I don't have to, is it my duty to stay home? And that's a war that's going on right now."

The Chase was released on September 22. Advance retail orders for the album approached four million, and many stores around the country opened at midnight for fans who couldn't wait another day. Joe Mansfield, the former Liberty vice-president of marketing who masterminded the promotional blitz for *Ropin' the Wind,* was hired by Doyle/Lewis management as a marketing consultant for *The Chase.* Liberty set the list price for the album at $16.98, making it the highest-priced, single-artist, standard-length CD on the market. (Subsequent releases by Michael Bolton and Madonna also carried a $16.98 list price.) *The Chase* contains about thirty-seven minutes of music. By contrast, Garth's eighty-five-minute home video, *This Is Garth Brooks,* sells for $24.95.

Garth said he wasn't worried about having two new albums out at the same time, since one was a seasonal release. But he admitted that he was concerned about how well *The Chase* would perform in the long run compared to *No Fences* and *Ropin' the Wind.* "I don't feel pressure coming from people as much as I do coming from me," he told Bruce Britt of the *Los Angeles Daily News.* "It's that competitive thing I grew up with. If *The Chase* doesn't sell as well as the other albums, does that make it a lesser album, and does it mean I'm on my way down? I don't know. I guess you just say your prayers and see what happens."

As the album's title suggests, Garth refuses to give up the chase, even when he's way ahead. There may be more talented singers and songwriters in Nashville, but no successful contemporary country artist consistently

John Paschal / Celebrity Photo

Garth arrives at the 27th Annual Academy of Country Music Awards with actress Sela Ward.

Garth wins top male vocalist and entertainer of the year at the 27th Annual Academy of Country Music Awards. With Sandy, in the early stages of her pregnancy.

Scott Downie / Celebrity Photo

takes more chances with style or content. Although some of the songs on *The Chase* recall Garth's previous work, he's not satisfied merely to repeat the formulas that have worked for him in the past. Garth himself describes *The Chase* as "very heavy, very intense. It starts intense and ends intense. In between it gets fun and light, but it's real."

The first single from the album, "We Shall Be Free," was written by Garth and Stephanie Davis in response to the Los Angeles riots. Garth introduces the song with the disclaimer, "This ain't comin' from no prophet/just an ordinary man . . ." Then with Donna McElroy's black gospel choir urging him on, the singer brings up various societal ills—world hunger, homelessness, racism, greed, environmental destruction, religious intolerance—and proposes that only when these problems are addressed shall we be truly free. Compared to the righteous anger and radical viewpoints common in rock and rap, it's pretty mainstream stuff, especially since Garth doesn't point a finger at anyone or offer specific political solutions. But for country music, often viewed as a bastion of conservative or reactionary attitudes, it's a daring statement—particularly the line about being ''free to love anyone we choose.''

Garth told *Billboard* that he is indeed defending the right to homosexual and interracial relationships. ''As long as you think the color of skin affects how someone can do their job, as long as you think who someone chooses to sleep with affects how they do their job, it's not a free country, it's an ignorant nation,'' he said. ''The fact that homosexuals feel they have to have individual rights is [due to] a direct failure of people to realize that we're all human beings. The fact that there is a word 'minority' represents [our] failure [to] realize we're all human beings.''

Garth had a hand in writing five of the album's ten songs. ''Mr. Right,'' only the second entirely self-written song Garth has recorded, is a lighthearted western-swing romp in which the singer advertises himself as either ''Mr. Right or Mr. Right Now.'' ''That Summer,'' cowritten with Pat Alger, tells the story of a hot-blooded teenage boy and a lonely young widow ''burnin' both ends of the night.'' The melody recalls Bob Seger's ''Night Moves''—sometimes covered by Garth in concert—and Trisha Yearwood adds sensuous harmonies. ''Somewhere Other Than the Night,'' cowritten with Kent Blazy, squanders one great verse and a tender message not to take love for granted on an overdone melodic arrangement reminiscent of ''What She's Doing Now'' on *Ropin'*. ''Every Now and Then,'' cowritten with Buddy Mondlock, has a pretty melodic hook and a persuasive pop-folk rhythm that recalls ''The River.'' But the theme of the song—sweet memories of love gone by—was depicted more arrestingly on ''Every Time It Rains'' on Garth's debut album.

As on all his albums, *The Chase* includes a western-underground cowboy song, Larry Burton's ''Night Rider's Lament,'' complete with a yodeling coda by Garth. ''Learning to Live Again,'' written by Stephanie Davis and Don Schlitz, is based on the instantly classic country refrain ''This learning to live again is killing me . . .'' The lyrics compassionately describe a nervous man, single again after many years, who finally realizes that his blind date is in exactly the same boat he is in.

From the outset of his career, Garth has declared his desire to combine the traditional country of the sixties with folk and rock influences from the seventies. He honors those sources at the center of *The Chase* with faithful covers of Patsy Cline's ''Walking After Midnight'' and Little Feat's ''Dixie Chicken.'' Garth's treatment of ''Walking'' doesn't improve on the original version, although it's wonderful that he's pointing young country audiences in Cline's direction. ''Dixie Chicken'' features sizzling lap steel guitar by Bruce Bouton and a slurred, wild-eyed vocal by Garth that should answer those critics who've accused him of lacking funk. Producer Allen Reynolds

Scott Downie / Celebrity Photo

John Paschal / Celebrity Photo

With the Judds, backstage at the 27th Annual Academy of Country Music Awards

said Garth showed up at Jack's Tracks Studios one day with a copy of Little Feat's live album and insisted they cut "Dixie Chicken." An FM rock radio staple twenty years ago, the song could become one of the biggest country hits of 1993 if Garth's instincts once again prove correct.

But while Garth clearly respects the lessons of the past, he's equally intent on broadening the lyrical focus of country music. On the disturbing yet redemptive set-closer, Tony Arata's "Face to Face," the singer takes a hard look around at the violence of the modern world and comes face to face with the devil inside—the fear of one's own mortality. The song's final refrain is " 'Cause it'll never go away until the fear that you are running from is finally embraced/Face to face . . ." Luke the Drifter, shake hands with Sigmund Freud and join the chase. We're going where no singer in a cowboy hat has gone before.

The Chase isn't flawless, but it is a more cohesive work than *Ropin' the Wind,* while still offering something for just about everyone in Garth's broad country constituency. The night of the album's release, Garth appeared on two network television shows, "Dateline" and "The Tonight Show." In an interview that apparently had been taped a few weeks earlier, Garth told

"Dateline" anchor Jane Pauley that he'd been unhappy in his work for the past year and a half, although he later admitted that he would always be "happy being unhappy, happy with the struggle." His eyes filled with tears when Pauley asked him what he hoped to be doing five years from now. "If I have my way, I'll be a good husband, a good father, and a good son to my folks," Garth replied. "Everything else is up in the air."

After the interview, Pauley half-seriously attributed Garth's emotional comments to "post-partum depression" and added, "He'll probably still be talking about quitting twenty years from now."

By the time he appeared on "The Tonight Show" on the evening of September 22, Garth appeared to be in much better spirits. He sang "We Shall Be Free" and "The Thunder Rolls" with his band and chatted amicably with host Jay Leno. When Leno asked him if he had a baby picture in his wallet, Garth at first demurred and then pulled out a huge photo of Taylor from behind his chair. "The way things are going, that'll fit in your wallet," cracked Leno. Then, to the surprise of no one in the music business, Garth announced that he had met with Joe Smith, president of Capitol's U.S. operations, who had persuaded him that premature retirement wasn't necessary. The 1993 tour would be postponed for eight months so the biggest star in country music could spend quality time at home with his family. Garth said he hoped that by late '93, Taylor would be old enough that she and Sandy could join him on the road.

Near the end of the interview, Leno asked how Sandy would react to having him around the house all the time. "I give her two or three months before she's plotting a way to kill me," Garth said with a sly grin. And millions of fans breathed a collective sigh of relief. Troyal Garth Brooks has knocked down fences and roped the wind, but the chase is not yet over.

THE GREATEST MUSIC IN THE WORLD

"We treat lyrics like the woman any man wants to impress the most. . . . I'm not sure other formats are remembering that the lyrics are what it's all about."

Between 1989 and 1991, the country recording industry roughly tripled its gross income, from around $500 million in sales of records, tapes, and CDs to an estimated $1.5 billion. Much of this increase is attributable to the impact of one man—Garth Brooks. Based on advance orders for *Beyond the Season* and *The Chase*, Brooks's total album sales should be at least 27 million by the end of 1992. No other popular music artist in this decade comes close to matching this figure—not Michael Jackson, not Madonna, not Hammer, not Guns N' Roses, not U2, not Michael Bolton, not Mariah Carey, not New Kids on the Block.

What does it mean for country music to have one of its own leading the pack for the first time in the history of American music? When *Ropin' the Wind* became the first country album ever to enter the pop chart at Number 1 in 1991, Capitol Records (now Liberty) threw a celebration in Nashville covered by *Country Music* magazine. "Sure, Garth Brooks is great for Capitol Records," said label head Jimmy Bowen. "But Garth Brooks is also great for all of Nashville and all of country music. . . . Garth Brooks has set a new benchmark, and you're going to see him continue to succeed because he's got his head on straight and he's got some very creative ideas on how to reach people. He's showing you how you act when you earn this kind of success. He's a fine young man."

Brooks's broad personal and musical appeal has demonstrated once and for all that country is not forever doomed to second-class status in the American music market. He's shown that country artists can compete with rock and pop at the highest levels, without sacrificing their country identity. "You want to know why country is so popular?" Brooks says. "It's because it's the greatest music in the world. I'm just glad people are starting to realize that."

But while Garth Brooks has been great for country music, country music also has been great for Garth Brooks. As Bill Ivey, director of the Country Music Foundation, points out, the groundwork for Brooks's massive success was laid by earlier generations of country artists, from Hank Williams and Patsy Cline to Willie Nelson and Emmylou Harris.

"I don't want to make him sound too calculated, because these are artistic decisions, but I think his instincts in terms of songs and performance style and how he relates to the audience are almost flawless," Ivey says. "I almost think he sat down five years ago and figured it out. He's kept himself country, and he either has picked or cowritten some really great songs. He has that high-energy, rockin' performance style that works in a huge venue. And he has a disarming candor in interviews and in addressing the public that helps people love him. To that extent, I think he's an innovator making this happen. But what he's doing would not work if Willie and Waylon, Emmylou, Ricky Skaggs, George Strait, and Randy Travis hadn't come first to put pieces of that puzzle out on the table."

From Ivey's historically based perspective, Brooks and other country artists of his generation are the beneficiaries of the gradual acceptance of authentic country music by the mass pop audience, which initially scorned country as the folk music of backward hillbillies.

"In the late 1940s, Hank Williams showed that great country songs could appeal to a wide audience, but they had to be performed by other people like Tony Bennett," Ivey says. "In the early sixties, artists like Jim Reeves and Patsy Cline and Eddy Arnold and Roger Miller showed that country artists could appeal to a broader pop audience, but they had to alter their style, or at least their appearance. Garth is a guy who is unashamedly country in his repertoire and his dress and his allegiances, but he appeals to a mass audience with all those country elements intact. I think he's done a great job of fusing a rock 'n' roll stage show with country songs and costuming. To me, that's Garth's role. He's the guy who's totally country but can attract a real mass audience. No matter what else happens to his career, I think he's going to be credited with playing that role."

Like other admittedly partisan observers in Nashville, Ivey believes country music could replace rock and roll as the foremost form of popular music in the nineties. "For a lot of reasons, country music works for the nineties," he says. "It's accessible. It's poetic. The baby boomers are getting to an age where their children are growing up. Music that speaks to the everyday concerns of grownups makes sense to a larger part of the population than it did ten or twenty years ago. I think we're coming, in a very natural way, to the end of the rock and roll era. I don't think we know yet precisely what will be next. But by the time the principal icon of a music that prides itself on being rebellious ends up on a postage stamp, you're probably more at the end of something than at the beginning. Rock had a great run for thirty-five to forty years, longer than the big band era. We're coming into something else. I think, in the short run, country is the beneficiary of this change."

While eulogies for the rock era probably are premature, part of country's current appeal undeniably is what it's *not*. It's *not* stupid and boring heavy metal; it's *not* ugly and one-dimensional punk-thrash; it's *not* musically minimalist and/or sexist rap; and it's *not* shallow neo-disco dance music. In many ways, country music in the nineties has more in common with the rock and roll of the fifties—and much of the rock of the sixties and seventies—than modern rock does.

Bowen caused a stir in some circles when he was quoted in *Time* magazine as saying, "Thank God for rap. Every morning when they play that stuff, people come running to us." Bowen—and, by extension, the entire country music industry in Nashville—was accused of catering to white racism in the *New York Times* op-ed section by veteran rock critic Dave Marsh.

Of course, Marsh launched his broadside attack before Brooks released "We Shall Be Free," a gospel song that unites black and white forms of Southern music with an uplifting message of brotherhood. "We Shall Be Free" might not speak to the concerns of urban black youth as directly as rappers Public Enemy or Ice Cube, nor is it likely to convert many David Duke supporters. But the song's success should prove to skeptical rock critics what country fans already knew: that there is nothing inherently racist about country music, and not everyone who wears a cowboy hat is a narrow-minded redneck.

Bowen's views on rap aside, it's not necessary for country music to justify itself—or to allow others to define it negatively—by what it is not. The music is valid enough on its own terms. Despite the formularized process of music-making in Nashville, nowhere else in the commercial pop landscape can you count on finding well-crafted songs with strong melodies and intelligible lyrics played by real musicians on real instruments. Where so much contemporary pop music is mainly about image and groove, country music is mainly about the *song*. As Brooks told *Forbes* magazine, "We treat the lyrics like the woman any man wants to impress most. We give the lyrics all the attention we can. I'm not sure other formats are remembering that the lyrics are what it's all about."

Country comes out of the same Afro-European melting pot as the rest of American music—blues, gospel, jazz, rock and roll, and rhythm and blues. Although country is thought of as the traditional music of white Southerners and Westerners, the music's great innovators—Jimmy Rodgers, Bob Wills, Hank Williams, Bill Monroe—all claimed they learned at least half of what they knew from black musicians. But where rock and R&B have been constantly pressing ahead, country tends to look to the past for its artistic inspiration. As Waylon Jennings memorably put it in a song, "Are you sure Hank done it this way?" Country always has been suspicious of rapid innovation, which has been both its strength and weakness. Country tends to run a decade or two behind the cutting edge of rock, which is why Garth Brooks singing a twenty-year-old Little Feat tune is hip. He's turned it into country music.

By the same token, country's deeply ingrained traditionalism has made it comparatively immune to pop's flavor-of-the-month trendiness (notwithstanding the occasional novelty crossover hit, such as Billy Ray Cyrus's "Achy Breaky Heart"). As MCA Nashville vice-president Tony Brown told Karen Schoemer of the *New York Times*, "Country music isn't like pop music. If it's rootsy it's too rootsy for pop radio, and if it's contemporaried-up a little bit, it sounds like a real bad version of pop music." Brown and others haven't forgotten the Urban Cowboy crossover era, when country music humiliated itself by pretending to be something it wasn't. The fad lasted a couple of years, after which the country industry was plunged into the worst slump in its history.

This is what makes the Garth Brooks phenomenon so encouraging. By mainstream country standards, Brooks is an innovator, and his music has been criticized at times for straying too far from a traditional country base. But Brooks obviously has learned from the mistakes of the Urban Cowboy era. While he's outselling everyone else in the marketplace, he hasn't done it by crossing over to the pop audience—he's made that audience come to him, and all of country music has benefitted from his stand.

Of course, as Brooks has observed, a growing number of perceptive and open-minded pop listeners can appreciate quality music of all kinds, whether it's Vince Gill or Bonnie Raitt or Luther Vandross. The artificial fences between country, rock, and R&B have been rebuilt since Chuck Berry and Elvis Presley knocked them down the first time thirty-five years ago. But Brooks told *USA Weekend* he can foresee a day when "There won't be country music, there won't be rap music, all the labels. It'll just be what sounds good and feels good to people. That's what they'll listen to, and the rest will fall by the wayside."

But until that day comes, Garth Brooks will dance with the ones who brung him to the ball. For the first time in its history, country is in the driver's seat of American music, and the guy behind the wheel is just an "old, fat, bald cowboy" from Oklahoma. Long may he run.

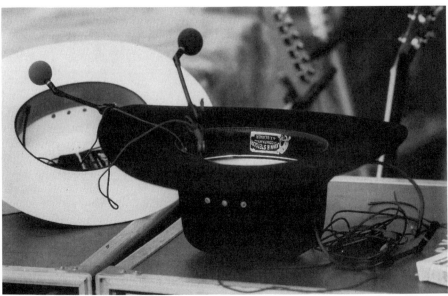

Steve Lowry

INDEX

ABOUT THE AUTHOR

Rick Mitchell covers country, jazz, and pop music for *The Houston Chronicle*. In the last ten years, his articles and reviews have appeared in dozens of regional and national publications, including *Request*, *Musician*, *Downbeat*, *Rolling Stone*, *The Los Angeles Times*, *LA Weekly*, *BAM*, *Willamette Week*, *The Oregonian*, and *The Bakersfield Californian*. He lives in Houston, Texas, with his wife, Lori, and daughter Chelsea Pearl.